I walked through a season of doubt in my life, and I would have given anything to have a guide like this through it! Thank you, Craig, for normalizing these struggles and not leaving people there but giving them handles and a way to connect with God in a deeper way through it.

—Jennie Allen, founder and visionary, IF:Gathering and Gather25; *New York Times* bestselling author

The Benefit of Doubt is a timely and much needed guide for anyone wrestling with questions of faith. Craig shows us how those questions and uncertainties can be pathways to a deeper relationship with God rather than a barrier to faith. Craig's wisdom, insight, transparency, and authenticity will encourage you to explore your faith, leading to a life of greater purpose and clarity.

—Christine Caine, founder, A21 and Propel Women

Craig Groeschel speaks to the saint and the cynic in *The Benefit of Doubt*. We all have questions, and Craig vulnerably opens the door for raw honesty and transformational faith to collide. Instead of feeling isolated in our doubts, or even rejected, *The Benefit of Doubt* brings clarity to our hearts' confusion and speaks peace as we continue to ponder. Your journey will be fortified and renewed as you carefully examine the God who relentlessly pursues us with patience and perfect love.

—Rich Wilkerson Jr., lead pastor, VOUS Church

Do you worry that your faith isn't strong enough? Craig Groeschel has written *The Benefit of Doubt* for you. Read it and see that doubts are nothing to fear—in fact, they can be your path to the rock-solid faith you've always wanted.

—Arthur C. Brooks, Harvard professor; #1 *New York Times* bestselling author

Having doubts about God is something almost everyone will experience. Those doubts either strengthen someone's faith or deconstruct it. In *The Benefit of Doubt*, Pastor Craig gives biblical insight to all the whys you may have about Christianity.

—Sadie Robertson Huff, author; speaker; founder, Live Original

Pastor Craig Groeschel has become a mentor to me and many in our church through his writing. His latest masterpiece, *The Benefit of Doubt*, teaches us that doubt is not a dead end but a doorway to deeper faith. This is a timely guide for anyone who wrestles with what they believe about God, and I have learned that everyone does at some point. So buy it for now or for later, and get a copy to give away. This book will help you turn your questions into your biggest spiritual-growth catalyst.

—**Jonathan Pokluda**, lead pastor, Harris Creek Baptist Church; bestselling author; host, *Becoming Something* podcast

It's not wrong or shameful to find yourself in the valley of doubt when you're faced with huge questions or hard circumstances. Craig Groeschel is a pastor, and even he has been there! He knows what it's like to be surrounded by shadows, and through this book, he shows you the way back to the light.

—**Lewis Howes**, *New York Times* bestselling author, *The School of Greatness* and *The Greatness Mindset*

Surprisingly, redirected doubt can actually deepen our faith rather than diminish it. *The Benefit of Doubt* is a compassionate guide to help each of us do just that. With honesty and transparency, Pastor Craig Groeschel tackles the tough questions we wrestle with when the obstacle of doubt presents itself, transforming it to a doorway of trust and transformation.

—**Lisa Bevere**, *New York Times* bestselling author; cofounder, Messenger International

In *The Benefit of Doubt*, Pastor Craig Groeschel confronts the most difficult questions we often wrestle with in our faith. I grew up believing that if I doubt, I have no true faith, yet I am reminded in this book that the strongest faith is not a faith that never doubts but rather a faith that perseveres through the doubts. When we stop feeling judged by our doubts and shamed by our questions, then we can begin to see that doubts can actually deepen our faith and lead us to know God more.

—**Madison Prewett Troutt**, bestselling author; podcast host; speaker

"Lord, I believe. Help my unbelief" is a deep and powerful response our Savior can use to draw all of us deeper. That's what Pastor Craig does in this fantastic book. God uses the honesty, stories, and Scriptures to draw us close to the heart of God.

—**Earl McClellan**, lead pastor, Shoreline City Church

Doubt is *not* a dirty word! Many believers have moments of doubt, and Pastor Craig's latest book, *The Benefit of Doubt*, does a masterful job attacking these realities head on. This book guides you through the (brave) process of allowing your doubt to serve as an invitation to deepen your faith. A timely must-read for today's modern era.

—**Stephanie Chung**, board member; speaker; author, *Ally Leadership: How to Lead People Who Are Not Like You*

In every question there is a quest! I'm grateful for how Pastor Craig reminds us of the hope we have in Jesus while navigating the daunting journey through our days of doubt.

—**Tim Tebow**, former professional athlete; five-time *New York Times* bestselling author; founder, Tim Tebow Foundation

This book hits home with straight truth as Craig tackles some of the toughest questions we all ask as believers. If you're looking for wisdom and a little gut check, this is it.

—**Willie Robertson**, CEO, Duck Commander; author; star, *Duck Dynasty*

ALSO BY CRAIG GROESCHEL

Altar Ego: Becoming Who God Says You Are

Chazown: Discover and Pursue God's Purpose for Your Life

The Christian Atheist: Believing in God but Living As If He Doesn't Exist

Daily Power: 365 Days of Fuel for Your Soul

Dangerous Prayers: Because Following Jesus Was Never Meant to Be Safe

Dare to Drop the Pose (previously titled *Confessions of a Pastor*)

Divine Direction: Seven Decisions That Will Change Your Life

Fight: Winning the Battles That Matter Most

*From This Day Forward: Five Commitments to Fail-
Proof Your Marriage* (with Amy Groeschel)

Hope in the Dark: Believing God Is Good When Life Is Not

Lead Like It Matters: Seven Leadership Principles for a Church That Lasts

*Liking Jesus: Intimacy and Contentment in a Selfie-
Centered World* (previously titled *#Struggles*)

Love, Sex, and Happily Ever After (previously titled *Going All the Way*)

The Power to Change: Mastering the Habits That Matter Most

Soul Detox: Clean Living in a Contaminated World

*Think Ahead: Seven Decisions You Can Make Today for
the God-Honoring Life You Want Tomorrow*

Weird: Because Normal Isn't Working

What Is God Really Like? (general editor)

Winning the War in Your Mind: Change Your Thinking, Change Your Life

CRAIG GROESCHEL

THE

BENEFIT

OF

DOUBT

HOW CONFRONTING YOUR DEEPEST QUESTIONS

CAN LEAD TO A RICHER FAITH

ZONDERVAN
BOOKS

ZONDERVAN BOOKS

The Benefit of Doubt
Copyright © 2025 by Craig Groeschel

Published in Grand Rapids, Michigan, by Zondervan. Zondervan is a registered trademark of The Zondervan Corporation, L.L.C., a wholly owned subsidiary of HarperCollins Christian Publishing, Inc.

Requests for information should be addressed to customercare@harpercollins.com.

Zondervan titles may be purchased in bulk for educational, business, fundraising, or sales promotional use. For information, please email SpecialMarkets@Zondervan.com.

ISBN 978-0-310-36987-5 (international trade paper edition)

Library of Congress Cataloging-in-Publication Data

Names: Groeschel, Craig, author.
Title: The benefit of doubt : how confronting your deepest questions can lead to a richer faith / Craig
     Groeschel.
Description: Grand Rapids, Michigan : Zondervan Books, [2025]
Identifiers: LCCN 2024028345 (print) | LCCN 2024028346 (ebook) | ISBN 9780310366621 (hardcover) |
     ISBN 9780310366676 (audio) | ISBN 9780310366638 (ebook)
Subjects: LCSH: Belief and doubt—Religious aspects—Christianity. | Spiritual life—Christianity.
Classification: LCC BT774.G83 2024 (print) | LCC BT774 (ebook) | DDC 248.4—dc23/eng/20240708
LC record available at https://lccn.loc.gov/2024028345
LC ebook record available at https://lccn.loc.gov/2024028346

Craig Groeschel is represented by Thomas J. Winters of Winters & King, Inc., Tulsa, Oklahoma.

Cover design: Faceout Studio / Tim Green
Cover images: Shutterstock
Interior design: Denise Froehlich

Printed in the United States of America

24 25 26 27 28 LBC 5 4 3 2 1

Contents

A Note from the Author ix

PART 1: DEALING WITH DOUBT

1. Is Doubt a Dead End? 3
2. Is There Life after Deconstruction? 21

PART 2: OUR DOUBTS

3. Why Should I Believe God Is Good? 43
4. Why Doesn't God Answer My Prayers? 61
5. Why Would God Provide Only One Way? 79
6. Why Believe in Jesus When His Followers Are Such Hypocrites? . . 95
7. Why Does God Feel So Far Away? 115
8. Why Would God Send People to Hell? 133
9. Why Believe the Bible If Science Contradicts It? 151
10. Why Would God Love Me? 167

Conclusion: Giving God the Benefit of the Doubt 181
Overview Exercise 189
Where Do I Go from Here? 191

Appendix: Encouraging Scriptures for Days of Doubt 193
Acknowledgments 205
Notes 207

A Note from the Author

I believe everyone—whether a long-term committed Christian or a long-term committed atheist—struggles with doubts. The doubts of a Christ follower can take the shape of benign curiosity or a malignant tumor. It seems more Christians today are struggling and questioning or deconstructing their faith.

I wrote this book because I understand and I want to help.

This may be the most personal book I've written. Not only do I open up about some of my deepest doubts and darkest spiritual fears, but I also share personal and intimate true stories of people I know and love. Several of their stories are raw and embody ongoing pain or unanswered questions. To honor the privacy and dignity of these people I love and pastor, I've chosen to occasionally use different names. I'm praying God continues to work in their lives and in yours.

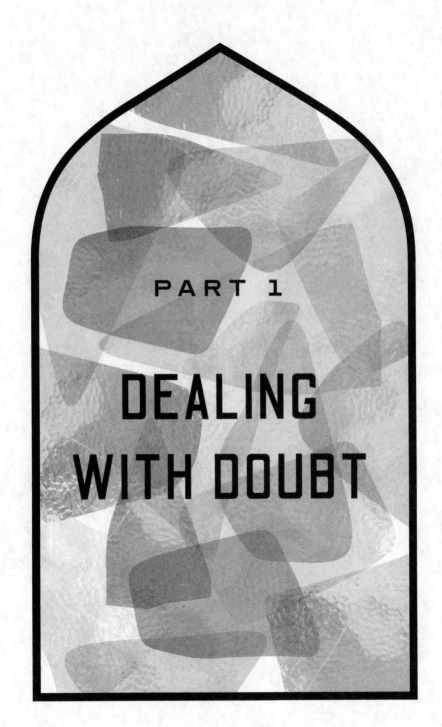

PART 1

DEALING WITH DOUBT

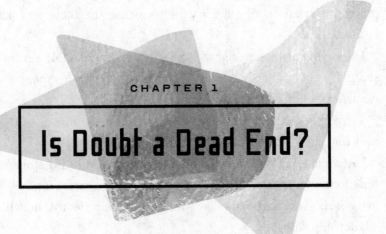

Is Doubt a Dead End?

I Doubted

"What if God isn't real?"

I never thought I'd ask that question.

Until I did.

But I didn't just ask, I shouted it at the top of my lungs, fighting back tears, while driving home in my 1985 dirty red Geo Prizm (which has been named the third-ugliest car ever made).

To be clear, while it certainly didn't help, the reason I plunged into doubt and spiritual despair wasn't because of the Geo Prizm.

I had resigned from a great job in business where I was making a lot of money to go into ministry where I wouldn't be making much at all. But I was excited to make the sacrifice, because my faith was on fire and all I wanted to do was serve Jesus and help people know him.

To add to my financial challenges, I was also paying my own way through seminary. Another sacrifice, but worth it. I felt that my education would help me grow in my faith, which would prepare me for pastoral ministry.

But, of all places, seminary was where I began my descent into a dark season of doubt and despair.

This will likely sound shocking to you, because it was to me, but I quickly discovered that my brilliant, well-respected *Bible* seminary professor—wait for it—did *not* believe that the Bible was inspired by God.

Yes, you read that right. My New Testament Bible professor in seminary—a higher-learning institution that trains people to be ministers—didn't believe the Bible.

Not only did he not believe, but he would make sure to tell us *every week* that the Bible was not the inspired Word of God.

At first I easily dismissed his statements. I'd heard stories about "intellectual" professors who believed they were too smart for God. Trying to ignore his constant challenge, I decided I wouldn't let this man hurt my relationship with God.

But, over time, as the semester wore on, my unshakable faith started to wobble. A small crack formed at the base of my spiritual foundation. Then it grew. After all, this guy was way smarter than I. He had a job teaching the Bible, so he had to know it better than all of his students, right? That nagging question made me wonder, *Maybe, just maybe, he is right and I am the one who is wrong.*

Often I would leave his class, get into my Geo Prizm for the ninety-minute drive home, and start crying. (No, I wasn't crying because I was embarrassed to drive my car, although, again, that didn't help.) I was so confused. I was distraught. I would shout toward heaven as I drove, "God, are you really there? Is all this faith stuff true? Can I actually trust the Bible? Am I devoting my life to someone I'm not even sure is real?"

My faith, which had been growing like crazy since the day I came to Jesus, felt as though it was dying.

Honestly, I was afraid.

If Christianity wasn't true, I couldn't pretend it was. I wasn't sure what to do, who I would become, or where I would end up. I had staked my entire future on my faith being real. In college, I had gone from spiritually lost to saved. In seminary, I felt lost again.

Some Doubted

Jesus died.

Jesus was buried.

Jesus rose from the dead.

In the New Testament we read about thirteen post-resurrection appearances of Jesus before he ascended to heaven. Some of the people he appeared to include the following:

- Women near his tomb (Matt. 28:8–10)
- Two men as they walked to Emmaus (Luke 24:13–35)
- Ten of the disciples (John 20:19–25)
- Five hundred people at one time (1 Cor. 15:6)
- A group of followers at a meal (after rising from the dead and all of this activity, he must have been hungry!) (Luke 24:41–43)
- The disciples when they were fishing and met with Peter on the beach (John 21:1–23)
- The disciples on a mountain (Matt. 28:16–20)

In that final appearance on the mountainside, the disciples went to meet Jesus as he had told them to do. Soon he would ascend to heaven. (Which had to be mind-blowingly cool to see. Did he do it step, step, fly, Superman-style? Or straight up into the sky, Iron Man–style? Was there a whoosh sound? I'll be honest, I really hope there was a whoosh sound.)

Before ascending, Jesus gave his disciples their divine assignment. Starting in Matthew 28:18, he told them to go into all the world to tell people everywhere the good news of what had happened, so everyone might know and follow him.

But just after the disciples showed up on the mountain and just before Jesus gave that great commission, there's a verse we can easily miss. It's a crucial three-word phrase. Matthew 28:17 says, "When they saw him, they worshiped him; but some doubted."

Have you ever noticed that before? Some worshiped, but some doubted.

"They" are the disciples. The same people who were seeing Jesus, again, risen from the dead. Reading this story today, it's easy to understand that they worshiped.

But wait! Some doubted?

I have some questions when I read this, don't you?

First, *Why write this?* I mean, it doesn't make the disciples look great. How could they doubt in this moment? They'd seen Jesus multiple times after he'd risen from the dead. Some of them had eaten with him. And now Jesus was standing directly in front of them all.

Even still, some doubted?

Why include this? Well, here's the answer: Matthew wrote that "some doubted" because, well, some doubted.

One of the many things I love about the Bible is that it wasn't written to make anyone look good or be convincing. Instead, Scripture offers an accurate account of what happened in history, and so, since some doubted, Matthew reported that some doubted. For him to write this down meant that they didn't just think about their doubts but they expressed them out loud. Or, at least, they confessed it later. How else would Matthew have known?

Second question: *Why is this phrase in the Bible?* Sure, it's true. But it's not as though everything that happened is reported in Scripture. It never mentions Jesus or any of the disciples going to the bathroom, but it's safe to assume they did (and, honestly, I don't mind some details like that being left out of the Bible). Not everything is mentioned, so why say that they doubted? I think because we need to hear the truth.

We need to hear that even Jesus' disciples had doubts because we, too, have doubts.

And because it's important that we see how Jesus responded to doubts. Notice what he didn't do:

- He didn't ask, in a disappointed tone, "After all I've shown you and taught you, why do you have doubts?"

- He didn't announce, "Okay, who's doubting? Because you're out! But for all you non-doubters, I've got a Great Commission for you!"
- He didn't clear up their doubts before sending them out.

Nope.

We read in verse 17 "some doubted" and in verse 18 Jesus gave *all* of them the mission of going out into the world to share the gospel and make disciples.

Even the doubters.

Why?

Because doubts don't make you a bad Christian. They make you human.

Doubts are a part of faith, and as we're going to see, they can actually invite us into a deeper place.

Jesus knew some doubted, but he sent them out anyway.

> **DOUBTS ARE A PART OF FAITH THAT CAN ACTUALLY INVITE US INTO A DEEPER PLACE.**

Jesus sends out people who have doubts because, if he didn't, he wouldn't have anyone to send out!

We all have doubts. I have certainly had mine.

We Doubt

After reading my Geo Prizm story (I mean, my seminary experience), you may have thought, *But, Craig, that was a long time ago. You were in your early twenties. You weren't a pastor yet. I bet you don't have doubts like that anymore.*

I wish.

Let me tell you about one Sunday morning in 2017. I was standing on the front row of our church service singing a worship song, minutes away from going up to preach. I realized in that moment that I felt nothing. By nothing, I mean

- I didn't feel God's presence,

7

- I didn't feel like preaching,
- I didn't feel that I had any faith.

Panic erupted in me as I thought, *What if all of this isn't real? What if it has all been just emotions? Some say religion is a crutch—what if they're right?*

I felt as if someone had knocked the breath out of me.

I wondered if the people near me could hear my heart pounding, because I was sure it was louder than the music.

I started shaking.

I began to cry.

That's when I noticed the exit sign.

I thought, *Maybe I could just leave? Just walk right out of church.*

The reality is that, for quite a while now, a *lot* of people have had those same feelings, those same questions, and have been heading for the exit, walking out of church. And they've not returned. I'll give you some numbers and disturbing research findings in the next chapter. But why?

Why are people leaving?

I think most don't have a problem with Jesus. He's hard not to like.

Instead, they have questions but feel as though they can't ask them, so they've found no answers.

Yet there *are* answers. But many people don't feel safe asking. They want to, but they're embarrassed or ashamed or insecure, thinking, *What if I'm the only one? What will people think of me?* They're afraid, and church may not seem like the safest place to express their doubts.

Some of those who have mustered up their courage and finally asked their questions have, too often, been met with bumper-sticker theology that dogmatically states, "The Bible says it. I believe it. That settles it."

Thanks.

Thanks a lot.

Many are left wondering whether there are any answers at all. And then, just as I did, they noticed the exit.

Perhaps doubts have left *you* wondering. Maybe that's exactly why you're reading this book.

As we begin this journey together, may I ask, What do you doubt?

Until you get clarity about what you're doubting, you'll feel confused instead of asking questions and getting answers that can satisfy you.

Are you asking:

- Is there a God?
- Is Jesus who he said he is?
- Who is God? Is he really Jesus? Or Buddha? Or Allah?
- Does science contradict some things in the Bible?
- Does faith in Jesus really change people?
- Does God really love you?
- Could God ever use someone like you?
- Why isn't God answering your prayers? I've had people tell me, "I prayed and prayed for my friend to be healed of cancer. I just knew God would do it, but he didn't. *That's* when I started to question."
- Why does God allow so much pain and suffering in the world? Such as when little girls are trafficked or innocent babies die in extreme poverty?
- Why is there weird stuff in the Bible? A talking donkey. A woman who turned into salt. A rod that turned into a snake. And then there's all of those scary images in the book of Revelation!
- Why are there so many controversies among Christians *about* the Bible, such as whether women can teach, or whether the Bible should be taught verse by verse or topically, or which is the right translation of the Bible to teach from? Oh, and about predestination and premillennialism and pre-algebra. (Okay, not pre-algebra. But it does seem as if Christians fight over *everything* these days. Why?!)
- Why did God make me drive a Geo Prizm, the third-ugliest car in history, after I committed to serve him? (Sorry, one of my own questions slipped in.)

While you're pondering what you doubt, you may also want to assess why. What's lurking behind your doubt? Consider the *why* behind the *what*.

Let's look at some common dynamics that can be at the source:

- **DOUBTS MAY BE DRIVEN BY CIRCUMSTANCES.** We may hate what's happening and feel as if there's no way a good God would allow something so bad, which leads us to wonder if maybe there is no God or he's just not as good as we were told.

- **DOUBTS MAY BE DRIVEN BY INTELLECT.** I've found that people are especially vulnerable to intellectual doubts if they don't know why they believe what they believe. Then when one day a friend poses a question or a teacher belittles what they believe, suddenly there's a fissure in their faith and the foundation starts to falter.

- **DOUBTS MAY BE DRIVEN BY EMOTION.** We may realize our faith is built almost entirely on feelings. Perhaps there is a euphoric experience when a person comes to Jesus. Then, after being emotionally pumped for a bit, eventually that spiritual high begins to wear off. Now panic sets in and the questions come: *Is my faith disappearing? What if I was never really a Christian in the first place?*

- **DOUBTS MAY BE DRIVEN BY OTHER PEOPLE.** Maybe someone has been around some hypocritical Christians, such as a loved and respected pastor who fell morally or a dad who supposedly loved Jesus until an affair came out. So the person decides, "If that is what Christians are like, then I think the whole thing must be a joke."

- **DOUBTS MAY BE DRIVEN BY A RELATIONSHIP WITH AN ABSENT OR ABUSIVE FATHER.** If you look at the most famous atheists of all time, many of them had absent or abusive fathers, including Karl Marx, Sigmund Freud, Bertrand Russell, Jean-Paul Sartre, Friedrich Nietzsche, and Albert Camus. I get it. I bet it's easy to conclude, *If this is what earthly fathers are like, I sure don't want a heavenly Father!*

- **DOUBTS MAY BE DRIVEN BY PERSONALITY.** Some people are just naturally more cynical or contrarian. That can make it more challenging to have faith or easier to rebel against a family or a culture founded on faith.

- **DOUBTS MAY BE DRIVEN BY DECISIONS.** When Christians make deliberate decisions to sin and keep sinning, they'll feel farther and farther from God. Why? Because sin separates us from God. Then this person is upset because God seems distant and may start to wonder, *Where is God? Why don't I feel his presence? Is he even real?* But the issue is not with God. It's with the choice to stubbornly cling to sin.

Did any of these resonate with you? The why behind the what?

Our doubts cannot be diffused until they are defined.

If you don't know what's behind your doubt, you may never experience the benefit of your doubt.

So what is your doubt all about?

What do you doubt, and why?

This might be a good time to pause your reading and put this book down. Take a moment to face your doubts and your hurts objectively and honestly.

Don't be afraid to press into your emotions.

Don't be scared to ask your questions.

Don't hold back.

Whatever your doubt and whyever you doubt, I want you to know that, despite the impression you got from a parent, a pastor, or a Mr. The Bible Says It So That Settles It, doubt is normal. Everyone doubts. Doubt is part of the human experience. And, yes, doubt is even a part of faith. We're going to talk about how doubts don't have to take you away from God. Your doubts can draw you closer to him.

Some think of faith as a destination, as in *Someday I will arrive. I'll have graduated. Like those perfect people who don't struggle with doubts the way I do. Someday I'll have perfect faith too.*

No.

THE STRONGEST FAITH ISN'T A FAITH THAT NEVER DOUBTS. RATHER, IT'S A FAITH THAT GROWS THROUGH DOUBTS.

Faith is a journey. You *don't* arrive. You'll never understand it all or move beyond having questions. What I hope you'll discover in the pages to come is that the strongest faith isn't a faith that never doubts. Rather, the strongest faith is a faith that grows through doubts.

Thomas Doubted

Thomas Jefferson wrote the Declaration of Independence.

Thomas Edison invented the light bulb.

Thomas Brady Jr. led his teams to seven Super Bowl victories.

Thomas Hanks' character said, "Life is like a box of chocolates."

Thomas Cruise felt the need, the need for speed.

Thomas in the Bible doubted.

Right? That is what he's famous for; he doubted.

He got his reputation from one of those post-resurrection appearances I referenced earlier. Actually, two of them.

On the day that Jesus appeared to ten of the disciples, Thomas was absent.

John 20:24–25 tells us, "Now Thomas (also known as Didymus), one of the Twelve, was not with the disciples when Jesus came. So the other disciples told him, 'We have seen the Lord!'"

Thomas' friends, the guys he had been following Jesus and doing life with for three years, told him, "We've seen the Lord! We've seen the Lord! We've seen the Lord!" (It's like when your kids annoy you from the back seat by repeatedly asking, "Are we there yet? Are we there yet? Are we there yet?" Or like my persistent friend who never stops inviting me, "Come to CrossFit! Come to CrossFit! Come to CrossFit!")

How did Thomas respond? "If you guys say it, I believe it. That settles it."

Nope.

The rest of John 20:25 says, "But he said to them, 'Unless I see the nail marks in his hands and put my finger where the nails were, and put my hand into his side, I will not believe.'"

That's why this guy is known as Doubting Thomas, not Need for Speed Thomas.

But I'm convinced Thomas gets a bad rap.

Sure, the other guys didn't doubt. You know why? Because they were *there*. Because they *saw* Jesus.

Personally, I relate to Thomas. And I respect him. Thomas was a realist. He wanted to be sure. He asked for some evidence. He wasn't going to settle for someone else's word. He wasn't going to bet his eternal life on blind faith. Oswald Chambers is often quoted as saying, "Doubt is not always a sign that a man is wrong. It may be a sign that he's thinking."

The huge takeaway from Thomas' story is that if you have ever felt guilty about doubting, don't. Sincere faith grows through doubts.

In fact, based on the Scriptures we just read, if you were to rank the disciples in terms of faith and spiritual strength, Thomas might be right toward the top.

Why?

For starters, "doubting" Thomas was willing to die with Jesus. We see it in John 11 after Jesus' friend Lazarus died. He had been dead for four days. (The King James Version says that after all that time he "stinketh.") In John 11:14–15, Jesus spoke to his disciples, "Lazarus is dead, and for your sake I am glad I was not there, so that you may believe."

Seems like no big deal except the religious leaders in Lazarus' area were looking for Jesus because they wanted to kill him. So when Jesus said "Let's go to him," all the disciples probably gulped. Except Thomas. John 11:16 says, "Then Thomas (also known as Didymus) said to the rest of the disciples, 'Let us also go, that we may die with him.'"

That is not a lack of faith.

That's bold, risk-it-all faith!

Thomas spoke up and revealed a tremendous commitment to Jesus that we don't see in any of the other disciples in that moment.

Another reason Thomas' faith impresses me is because he kept showing up, even with his doubt. Remember, in John 20:25 the disciples insisted "We have seen the Lord!" and Thomas told them he wasn't buying it. The next verse says, "A week later his disciples were in the house again, and Thomas was with them" (v. 26). Even in the middle of his doubt, even when he wasn't sure, Thomas still showed up. *That's* faith. That's commitment.

If you're wrestling with doubts, deciding to read this book shows your faith. I commend you on your commitment even while you have questions. I commend you on your commitment especially if you have questions.

And how did Jesus respond to Thomas' doubt?

He found him.

He came to him.

Jesus entered the room and said, "'Peace be with you!' Then he said to Thomas, 'Put your finger here; see my hands. Reach out your hand and put it into my side. Stop doubting and believe.' Thomas said to him, 'My Lord and my God!'" (John 20:26–28).

Thomas had said that for him to believe he needed to see the nail marks and put his finger in the holes left from the crucifixion. Jesus came to Thomas and gave him exactly that! Amazing that he offered Thomas the *exact* evidence he asked for.

Jesus came close to Thomas and told him to touch his wounds. And what does that tell us?

God is not distant in your doubts.

When you've wondered about him and struggled with complicated questions, you might feel as though God is far off, perhaps as if you've pushed him away or maybe he has walked away from you.

GOD IS NOT DISTANT IN YOUR DOUBTS.

No.

He comes into the room with you.

He is willing to be touched.

So reach out to him.

You'll find that he's reaching out for you.

If you have questions, if there's something you're struggling to believe, tell him.

Thomas asked questions.

Jesus gave him answers.

The story of Thomas shows us that Jesus invites us to be honest with him.

And Thomas went on to declare Jesus "my Lord and my God" (v. 28) and to serve Jesus faithfully. Christian tradition tells us that Thomas obeyed Jesus' command to go and make disciples by traveling from place to place preaching the gospel. Finally, in India, he was told he would be killed if he wouldn't renounce his faith in Jesus. But that's something Thomas would not do. As he told his friends, "Let us also go, that we may die with him." By that point, his faith was far too strong to walk back the truth he had experienced. So his persecutors drove a stake through his stomach and murdered him.

Thomas lived and died for Jesus. Because, in the middle of his doubt, Jesus showed up.

And that's what I believe he will do for you. No matter what questions you are asking and no matter how loud your doubts shout, you can find the courage to take them to Jesus—for the first time or the hundredth time.

As we journey through the pages of this book, we may not find perfect answers to every question. And we may not be able to cleanly resolve every doubt. But with all my heart, driven by my own experience of dealing with questions about faith, I believe Jesus will show up.

Let me repeat: your doubt doesn't mean God is distant.

This is what we will learn as we journey together:

- **YOUR DOUBT DOESN'T DISAPPOINT GOD.** When you experience confusion in your faith, your spiritual enemy, the devil, will try to use doubt to drive you away from God. He'll tell you things like God doesn't want anything to do with you. That's a lie. God knows you're human and that doubt is part of the journey of faith.
- **YOUR DOUBT DOESN'T DEFINE GOD.** The devil will insinuate that your unanswered questions expose the truth about God. To your question "Why is God not answering my prayer?" your spiritual

enemy will tell you, "Because he's not a God who wants to help you." When you ask, "Why is there so much evil in the world?" the devil will answer, "Because God isn't good." Once again, lies. Remember that your doubt does not define God.

- **YOUR DOUBT DOESN'T DEFINE YOU.** The devil will whisper that your doubt means you don't really have faith. That you're not a real believer. That's not true. We'll see that the heroes of the faith throughout the Bible experienced doubts along the way.
- **YOUR DOUBT DOESN'T DENY YOUR FAITH.** What I experienced during my drive home from seminary, as well as on that difficult Sunday morning standing in a worship service wondering whether God was real, was not a denial of my faith. I believe those experiences were ultimately about him inviting me to a deeper faith. He's doing the same in your life.
- **YOUR DOUBT DOESN'T DISQUALIFY YOU.** Remember, "some doubted," but Jesus sent them out anyway. The disciples' doubt didn't disqualify them. In fact, Jesus gave those doubters the greatest mission in the world!

All the things we're afraid doubt does—no, doubt *doesn't*.

When You Doubt

Now let me tell you the rest of my Sunday-morning story, when I was worshiping—okay, I wasn't worshiping, I was freaking out. I felt as if the light of God had gone out and I had fallen into a dark shadow. As the panicked questions flooded my mind, the siege of doubt was too much. Sitting there shaking, with my head in my hands and starting to cry, just before I was about to walk onstage to preach, I prayed a desperate prayer, "God, if you're there, show me something."

At that moment, I had the closest thing to a vision I've ever experienced.

I saw myself back in college reading in the Gospels about Jesus. I'd never really understood that he loved broken people like me. I remembered hitting my knees and calling out to God. I thought about when I first came to faith. Learning that it's only by grace through faith that you're made right with God.

The word that kept coming, overwhelming me in those memories? *Faith.*

Yes, I have doubts, but I still have faith.

And what I need is faith.

I realized that faith is not the absence of doubt.

Doubt is an invitation to a deeper faith.

And faith is the means to push through doubt.

This same connection is true in so many aspects of Christianity. Experiencing Christ's peace doesn't mean we will escape the chaos in our world. Receiving his love doesn't mean we won't struggle in getting along with the people around us. Partaking in his joy doesn't mean we will never have a bad

> DOUBT IS AN INVITATION TO A DEEPER FAITH.

day. What it does mean is that Jesus is with us in the midst of the day-to-day struggles in our lives. So just like peace, love, and joy, faith is there when the doubts come. It's not if but when.

As I remembered those early days of knowing Jesus, Psalm 23 came to mind: "Even though I walk through the valley of the shadow of death, I will fear no evil, for you are with me" (v. 4 ESV). That's how I felt, as though I were in the valley of the shadow of death. I asked myself, *What do you do when you're in a valley? How do you get through it?* You keep walking. On that Sunday morning, I realized I was in the valley not of the shadow of *death* but of *doubt.* And I wouldn't stay there. I would keep walking, in faith. Doubt would not be a dead end. This would not be my destination. I had faith, and with God's guidance and courage, I would emerge with a deeper faith.

If you're in the valley of doubt, keep walking. He is with you. As Jesus encouraged us in Matthew 7:7–8, keep asking, keep seeking, and keep knocking.

And keep reading, because in this book we'll examine and think through some questions many of us wrestle with:

- What should I do when I doubt God's goodness?
- Why doesn't God answer my prayers?
- Why would God provide only one way to him and heaven?
- A lot of Christians are hypocrites, and some have let me down, so why would I want to be one?
- Why does God sometimes feel so far away?
- What about the fact that I don't believe God could ever work through someone like me?
- Doesn't science disprove the Bible?
- How can I love God when I don't believe he loves me?

I believe that together we're going to find that there are authentic answers for these difficult questions.

I know you can emerge on the other side of this book with a deeper faith. It may not be easy. But it will be worth it. How do I know?

In that Sunday-morning worship service, I asked, "God, if you're there, show me something," and he showed up in the most powerful way.

I am convinced that if you approach the truths in this book with an open spirit, if you sincerely ask God, he will show up. Just as he did for me. Just as he did for Thomas.

Seek him and you will find him.

Or, even better, he will find you.

Doubt is not a dead end.

> **Be merciful to those who doubt.**
> —JUDE 22

CHAPTER 1 EXERCISE

1. Take some time to write out your doubts and questions regarding your faith. (Don't hold back. Be honest. You can use the bulleted list of common questions from this chapter as prompts.)

2. Why do you think evidence or experience (knowing the disciples had plenty of both) doesn't always answer every question in matters of faith?

3. How do you feel about the phrase "some doubted" being included in the story about the disciples gathered on the mountain before Jesus gave the Great Commission?

4. Why do you suppose so many people feel as though their doubts make them a "bad Christian"?

5. How did my Sunday-morning meltdown about my own doubts make you feel about your struggles with faith? How can you relate?

6. Consider the factors I listed that can drive doubt— circumstances, intellect, emotions, other people, fathers, personalities, or decisions. Did any of these resonate with you? Explain.

7. Was Jesus' response to Thomas encouraging to you? Explain.

8. Why do you think we tend to equate doubt with distance from God?

9. In the list of "Your doubt doesn't . . ." did any of those resonate with you? Explain.

10. What is your biggest takeaway from chapter 1?

Is There Life after Deconstruction?

I love conversion stories. Stories of people moving from unbelief to belief, or from doubt to faith. I celebrate every time I hear one.

But these days I'm hearing more frequent stories of people moving in the opposite direction, from belief to unbelief, from faith to doubt.

You don't have to scroll for long on social media or YouTube or through the news headlines to hear about young people leaving the church and "deconstructing their faith." This trend has gained enough momentum to be called "the deconstruction movement." In 2022, Lifeway Research released an article that places these deconstructionists into one of three categories:

1. They're walking away from their faith.
2. They're still committed to God but wrestling with the failing or sinful ways of religious institutions.
3. They're experiencing spiritual burnout from constantly being a doer in the church.[1]

Throughout the article, which includes statistics from Barna Research, one word recurs as a constant theme: doubt.

But why is this becoming increasingly common? Some suggest that it's almost trendy, but I think that's a gross oversimplification and ignores the deeper pain of those questioning their faith. Chances are you know some people (or may be one yourself) who would say things like this:

- "No one could give me adequate answers to the theological questions I was asking" (Emily, age 19).
- "After my pastor 'fell morally,' I just couldn't continue to trust in the God he proclaimed" (Steve, age 32).
- "I grew up believing in Jesus. But after watching the hate-filled actions of so-called Christians in the news and on social media, I don't want anything to do with that" (Ashley, age 23).
- "My parents claimed to be devout Christians. But their 'Christianity' is more of a toxic cocktail of their version of the Bible mixed with politics in ways Jesus never intended" (Cayden, age 23).
- "After God allowed me to be abused, I'm not able to reconcile the pain I endured with the existence of a loving God who cares" (Jenna, age 28).

My heart breaks every time I hear one of these stories.

What hurts so much is that these are not just random people. For me, it's personal. I have six kids who grew up with some incredible friends whom I love as my own. Most were in our house much of the time they were all growing up. Some even call me Dad. A few love Jesus and are faithfully serving him today, but others experienced hurts, had doubts along the way, and couldn't find answers. So rather than pursue a growing relationship with God, they chose to walk away from their faith.

Knowing that, I hurt for them.

I want to tell you what I *do* tell them when given the opportunity: Go ahead and deconstruct your faith. But do so with the intention of *reconstructing* a faith that is personal, credible, and beautiful. The good news is that there is a healthy, faith-building way to wrestle with sincere doubts.

Typically, this process happens in three stages of spiritual maturity. When done right, they can all be beneficial for everyone. An example of where we can see all three is in the life of the disciple Peter.

Stage 1: Construction

Before Peter followed Jesus, he was a fisherman named Simon. Peter's brother Andrew encountered Jesus first, then brought Peter to meet him (John 1:35–42). Immediately, Jesus changed his name from Simon to Peter, which seems a little forward, right? (I mean, I like giving people nicknames, but not usually the moment I meet them.)

Later, Peter was likely at the temple in Capernaum when Jesus gave one of his first sermons (Luke 4:31). Then he witnessed Jesus miraculously heal the sick, including Peter's mother-in-law in his own home (Luke 4:33–44). Soon, Jesus provided Peter a miraculous catch of fish and then called him to be one of his disciples (Luke 5:1–11).

All this time, Peter's faith was being constructed.

Your faith was constructed too.

I've told you about those early days in college when my faith was in this stage.

Think of it like building a house, except it's a faith house. You take the materials from everything you learn—Bible readings, sermons you hear at church, conversations with friends, your spiritual experiences—and build your understanding of God and the Christian life.

This lens you learn to see through is known as your worldview, which for the Christian means seeing the world through God's eyes by faith, not sight. Maybe when you look at your faith house, you feel pretty good about what you've built. It seems right, sound, and sturdy. Maybe you can't imagine how it could be any better.

But there are cracks in your construction that you just can't see yet.

Why? Because what you were taught wasn't perfect. And some conversations with friends may have led you to believe that some lies were truth. Maybe you came to have a simplistic understanding that couldn't handle the pressures of real life. Or you had emotional responses to experiences that felt right but didn't prepare you to mature into a more "grown up" faith. It's as though you constructed your faith house on a foundation with some cracks of faulty beliefs.

That's to be expected because, as flawed people, we all have some cracks in our foundation.

And when those cracks are exposed, it leads to doubt, and sometimes to a crisis of belief. But where do the cracks come from?

- **OURSELVES.** We may be the ones who bring faulty beliefs into the construction of our faith. Peter was being taught by Jesus and experiencing life with Jesus himself, so he couldn't possibly have cracks in his construction, right? Wrong. Peter did, because of prior beliefs he had and held on to. Peter believed God was only for Jewish people. As with so many others in that day, he believed the Messiah would be a political ruler who would lead a revolution to give the Israelites back their land as well as control over the government. Those beliefs were wrong, and when they crashed into the realities of who Jesus was and what he came to do, it led Peter to a crisis of belief. His faith was shaken.
- **OTHERS.** Others may also bring faulty beliefs into the construction of our faith. When we base our faith on someone else's mixed-up beliefs, it eventually brings trouble. This is what happened to Philip Yancey in his dark seasons of doubt. Yancey is a Christian author whose writings have helped to strengthen the faith of countless people. Two of his books—*The Jesus I Never Knew* and *What's So Amazing about Grace?*—have won the ECPA Christian Book Award. That's who Yancey is today, but there was a time in his past when he walked away from the faith he had always embraced. Why?

Yancey grew up with an overbearing Christian mother in an extremely legalistic church. He writes of his upbringing, "My earliest memories all involved fear."[2] His father died when he refused treatment for polio because he was convinced God would heal him and therefore didn't need drugs or doctors. Yancey was taught that a Christian couldn't watch TV, play cards, listen to secular music, go bowling or roller skating or to the movies or the opera, be in the same swimming pool as members of the opposite sex, or read the Sunday paper. His mother told him that to be in God's will he had to go to Bible college and become a missionary. There, he was taught that translations other than the King James Version were "godless, depraved crap"[3] and was forced to participate in the burning of secular record albums.[4] The Bible college he attended forbade women from wearing pants, except during certain activities when they could wear slacks—under a skirt.

Yancey finally reached a point where he couldn't just continue believing what he had always believed. He rightly questioned the naive faith of his childhood. Was everything he had been taught right? What was true and what wasn't?

What do you do when you realize the faith you've constructed from someone else's beliefs doesn't prove to be as right, sound, or sturdy as you assumed?

You deconstruct.

Stage 2: Deconstruction

So what if you discover your house has some issues? Some wood is rotten or there's a crack in the foundation. The house you were proud of, that made you feel secure, that was an extension of who you are, isn't quite what you thought it was.

What do you do now?

When that house is your faith, you deconstruct.

At the beginning of this chapter, I gave you some research data about deconstruction. As a pastor, I've increasingly had my own experiences with this over the past several years as I've talked with so many people about their faith-related questions.

Here are some different definitions for you:

- Deconstruction means abandoning all things Christian—becoming an agnostic or atheist.
- Deconstruction means staying committed to Jesus but abandoning religious institutions and churches, or at least those that don't live up to the teachings of Jesus as they see them.
- Deconstruction means continuing in a life of devotion to Jesus and participation in the church while rejecting a lot of the related cultural and political issues.

Here's an even simpler definition, which seems consistent with how Jesus ministered to people: Deconstruction is a spiritual journey during which a Christian examines his or her faith to release what's contrary to God's heart and embrace what's true.

To be clear, deconstruction done poorly can leave a wake of spiritual carnage. Like I said, I have witnessed it personally. On the other hand, I have also seen that deconstruction done well can be spiritually beneficial. Not only do I think deconstruction can be positive but also I offer that sometimes it's necessary. Just ask Peter, or Philip Yancey.

You could even make the case that, at times, Jesus was helping people deconstruct their faith.

For instance, in Matthew 5:43, Jesus says, "You have heard that it was said, 'Love your neighbor and hate your enemy.'" Everyone listening would have thought, *Yes, I have heard that. Not only have I heard it, I like it! And I live by it! If they're nice, be nice back, but if they're not, slit their chariot wheels when they're not looking!* Jesus continues in Matthew 5:44, "But I tell you, love your enemies and pray for those who persecute you."

Jesus was deconstructing their belief system. He was helping them see that what they believed was not true to God's heart or his kingdom's values. Five times in Matthew 5, Jesus says, "You have heard it said, but I say . . ." He was essentially saying, *Let's tear down your incorrect beliefs so we can build new beliefs that* are *true.*

Jesus did this with Peter, again and again.

Let's look at a few of those stories through the lens of faith and doubt.

In Matthew 14, Peter and the other disciples were in a boat at night when Jesus came walking out toward them on the water (which is *cool*). The disciples freaked out (which seems appropriate).

Matthew 14:26 says, "When the disciples saw [Jesus] walking on the lake, they were terrified. 'It's a ghost,' they said, and cried out in fear."

Jesus responded, "It is I. Don't be afraid" (Matt. 14:27).

I love that Jesus didn't say "It is I, Jesus." He just said, "It is I." Peter knew that when some dude comes at you *walking on water*, as soon as you establish that it's not a ghost, you know it's got to be Jesus.

The same Peter, who struggled with impulse control and very possibly had ADD and I'd guess was an Enneagram 8, if you're into that kind of thing, responded to finding out that the "ghost" was actually Jesus not by breathing a sigh of relief or giving an embarrassed smile or canceling his submission to *Ghost Hunters*. Instead he said, "Lord, if it's you . . . tell me to come to you on the water" (Matt. 14:28).

Jesus responded with a single word: "Come."

"Then Peter got down out of the boat, walked on the water and came toward Jesus" (v. 29).

I wonder whether Peter hurried out of the boat with great confidence or tiptoed out, testing his footing to make sure this crazy idea was going to work. It doesn't matter, because however he did it, he did it. He got out of the boat and became only the second man to ever walk on water. (I believe he is still one of only two.)

Faith is what led Peter from watching to walking on water. But doubt is what led Peter from walking to sinking: "But when he saw the wind, he was afraid and, beginning to sink, cried out, 'Lord, save me!' Immediately Jesus reached out his hand and caught him. 'You of little faith,' he said, 'why did you doubt?'" (vv. 30–31).

I love Jesus' question. He invited Peter to examine his beliefs and be honest about his doubts. To ponder why he thought the circumstances he was facing were bigger than the God he was trusting. To ask himself, *What if Jesus really is who he says he is and not who I assume he is?*

In Matthew 16, Jesus announces he is going to Jerusalem, where he'll be killed. But "Peter took him aside and began to rebuke him" (v. 22). (Anytime you find yourself rebuking Jesus, chances are very good that your theology is flawed.) Peter said, "This shall never happen to you!" (v. 22). Why was he being so strong about Jesus' words? Because Peter still embraced the common belief that the Messiah would be a conquering, political king.

How did Jesus respond in that moment? Roll his eyes and walk away, chuckling and muttering to himself, *That Peter is muy loco*? No. "Jesus turned and said to Peter, 'Get behind me, Satan! You are a stumbling block to me; you do not have in mind the concerns of God, but merely human concerns'" (v. 23). Then Jesus said, "Whoever wants to be my disciple must deny themselves and take up their cross and follow me" (v. 24). Jesus was direct. Why? He was loving and discipling Peter—helping him to let go of wrong human beliefs and grab on to a godly, right way of thinking. Jesus was helping Peter deconstruct his false belief system so he could replace it with a true biblical belief system.

Pastor and author Randy Frazee talks about the importance of allowing people to openly express their doubts inside the Christian community: "We should invite this confession of unbelief. In my experience, the journey of belief from head to heart is always coupled with and fueled by a season of doubt in which a person is making a decision to embrace or reject the faith of others, such as parents. We need to create an environment in the home and the church where they are encouraged to speak their doubts out loud. When they do, our response should be, 'Great! We were looking forward to this day.' With the mouth being halfway from the head to the heart, the confession of unbelief or doubt means the person is also halfway to truly owning their personal faith."[5] If doubts are allowed to leave the mind and be expressed through the release valve of the mouth, they are more likely to not seep into the heart and poison the believer's faith.

Something powerful happens when we're honest about our doubts, spiritual questions, and disappointments. God does something special when we take what's hidden in the darkest part of our hearts and expose it to his light.

> SOMETHING POWERFUL HAPPENS WHEN WE'RE HONEST ABOUT OUR DOUBTS, SPIRITUAL QUESTIONS, AND DISAPPOINTMENTS.

We would be wise to find the courage to express and examine our beliefs to see if they line up with God's Word. We may assume our beliefs all come from the Bible, but that's probably not as true as we think. Too often we subconsciously absorb our beliefs from other people or from our church or culture, then assume they're from the Bible.

Even when we go straight to Scripture, we can't help but read it through our own filters, such as these:

- Our family background and how we were raised
- Our circumstances, challenges, opportunities, or trials
- Our personality and our biases
- The teachings of the church we grew up in or now attend

While many of our beliefs about God are probably true and biblically accurate, because we're flawed people who learn from flawed people, we've also picked up some flawed ideas along the way.

For example, you may wrongly believe any of the following:

- **GOD WILL NEVER GIVE YOU ANYTHING YOU CAN'T HANDLE.**
  When you experience something in life you can't handle, you feel as if God hasn't been true to his promise. But God never promised that! This often gets confused with what Paul tells us in 1 Corinthians

10:13, "[God] will not let you be tempted beyond what you can bear." He talks about temptation, not life circumstances.

- **IF YOU NAME IT, YOU CAN CLAIM IT. GOD WILL ALWAYS GIVE YOU ANYTHING YOU ASK FOR!** This *is* based on Bible verses but an incomplete and inaccurate understanding of them. For example, John 15:7 is one often used in this teaching: "If you remain in me and my words remain in you, ask whatever you wish, and it will be done for you." Besides the qualifying phrases of "if you remain in me and my words abide in you," the context of John 15 is Jesus' teaching that we are the branches and God is the vine. Verse 5 is crucial: "Apart from me you can do nothing." Focusing only on "ask whatever you wish, and it will be done for you" is like hearing one sound bite out of an interview.

- **AS A CHRISTIAN, YOU HAVE TO BELONG TO THIS POLITICAL PARTY, WHICH IS GOD'S POLITICAL PARTY, AND THE PEOPLE WHO BELONG TO ANY OTHER ARE NOT TRUE CHRISTIANS.** The problem is that Jesus did not come to establish a political kingdom. And that *all* parties have some policies and ideologies that are true to God's heart and others that are antithetical to God's heart. In the days of Jesus' ministry, there were essentially two political parties—the Pharisees and the Sadducees. Throughout the Gospels, he showed no partiality toward either. Yet, to one curious Pharisee, Jesus did say in John 3:16–17, "For God so loved the world that he gave his one and only Son, that whoever believes in him shall not perish but have eternal life. For God did not send his Son into the world to condemn the world, but to save the world through him." "Whoever believes" and "the world" is clearly his invitation to anyone in *any* party.

- **GOD WANTS YOU HAPPY. HE LOVES YOU, AND HIS GREATEST JOY IS YOUR HAPPINESS.** This sounds good! And it is true! But only in part. God *does* love you, which is why his highest purpose is not your happiness but your holiness. And if your pursuit of happiness trips up your pursuit of holiness, then it's not God's will. To quote our water walker after his faith had been reconstructed, "But just as he who called you is holy, so be holy in all you do; for it is written: 'Be holy, because I am holy'" (1 Peter 1:15–16).

Or, like Philip Yancey, you may have grown up in a church that twisted the Bible to support racism or the claim that bowling, movies, and pants on women are sinful.

Then one day you wake up and realize everything you believe may not be biblical. Therefore, it may not be true.

Or, worse, you *don't* realize that it's not biblical, but you *do* realize that it's not true. And now what do you do? Do you have to chuck your faith? Do you walk away from Jesus?

No.

You don't.

You deconstruct. You let go of what's not true.

You reconstruct. You hold on to what is true.

Too often, instead of throwing out the bad and keeping the good, people throw everything away, even the parts that are true. Finally, what they're left with is nothing. Or, sadly, they become toxic and bitter. Now they have to figure out how to navigate life without any real foundation or framework.

At first it might feel freeing. You're not confined to your old house anymore! My son-in-law James Meehan is one of the primary communicators to the young people in our church, and he helped my thinking for this chapter. James says it this way: "The empty spot where your 'house' used to be will make you feel empty on the inside too." Why? Because instead of deciding to reconstruct your belief system by finding what is true and beautiful, you took a wrecking ball to it and lost the entire thing.

But there is good news.

Really good news.

Jesus was a carpenter.

And carpenters know how to build.

Stage 3: Reconstruction

Peter and the other disciples were probably cowering in a room together, afraid that at any moment soldiers might burst in and do to them what they had done to Jesus a couple of days before.

The man they had believed to be the Messiah, the one they thought would lead a revolution and liberate the Israelites from Rome, had been crucified. It didn't make sense. The reality they were experiencing could not coexist with what they believed about God and expected him to do.

Jesus was dead, and so was their faith.

And they had *no idea* what was about to happen. Because, minutes later, three women—Mary Magdalene, Joanna, and Mary, the mother of James—would come bursting into the room telling them that Jesus had risen. They had seen him. Peter would be racing to an empty tomb (Luke 24:1–12).

They learned something that day that would become a crucial part of their message for the rest of their lives—without a death there can be no resurrection. On the other side of Jesus' death, and the collapse of their faith, there was resurrection.

I hope you experience the other side of deconstruction: *reconstruction*. Why? Because there has been a resurrection!

My son-in-law James points out that when Jesus appeared again to the disciples, he still had his scars. His old body was not thrown away; it was made new. This is the beauty of our faith. God doesn't throw out the old to bring in the new. God makes old things new (2 Cor. 5:17; Rev. 21:5).

YOU CAN'T HAVE A RECONSTRUCTION OF YOUR FAITH WITHOUT A DECONSTRUCTION OF YOUR BELIEFS.

The disciples never fully understood Jesus or what he was about until after the resurrection. They first had to experience the pain of having their hope shattered and their faith broken.

Because you can't have a resurrection without a death.

And you can't have a reconstruction of your faith without a deconstruction of your beliefs.

Tearing Down and Building Up

In Matthew 7:24–27, Jesus used his experience as a carpenter to give an example for how to construct our lives with faith. As you read this passage, think about the rain as experience with suffering, the rising streams as conflicting questions, and the winds as doubts:

> "Therefore everyone who hears these words of mine and puts them into practice is like a wise man who built his house on the rock. The rain came down, the streams rose, and the winds blew and beat against that house; yet it did not fall, because it had its foundation on the rock.
>
> "But everyone who hears these words of mine and does not put them into practice is like a foolish man who built his house on sand. The rain came down, the streams rose, and the winds blew and beat against that house, and it fell with a great crash."

Jesus tells us that hearing his words and practicing them is the best way to build our faith house.

One of Jesus' ancestors, Solomon, told us there is "a time to tear down and a time to build" (Eccl. 3:3). The truth is, it's easier to tear down. It's harder to build something meaningful. Just watch any of the home-reno shows on TV. The "time to tear down" sledgehammer scene is a minute or two. Most of the episode focuses on the "time to build up."

As we deconstruct, are we questioning the validity and value of what we used to believe recklessly or carefully? Are we looking for what is true and good so we can keep it? Or are we just burning the whole thing down?

I'll give you an example. Three of my four daughters have serious health challenges. It's been heartbreaking and extremely confusing. We eventually discovered that the two side-by-side rooms they grew up in for their entire childhoods were infested with a dangerous toxic mold.

Did we nuke the house? No. If the whole house had been dangerous, we might have. But it wasn't the whole house, it was only two rooms.

So what did we do?

We deconstructed those two rooms.

We got rid of what was toxic.

We kept what was good and we tore out the bad, rebuilding it with something better.

When you realize that parts of your faith aren't true—aren't personal or credible or beautiful—you don't discard your faith. You discard the parts that aren't true.

And you do some rebuilding.

That's what Philip Yancey did. Piece by piece, he deconstructed his faith, and thank God he did. If not, he would still believe that Sunday papers, pop music, and card games are of the devil.

After all he went through, it would have been so easy for Yancey to reject his faith, but he didn't. He *deconstructed* his faith and then *reconstructed* his faith. He built a new and stronger faith based not on what his mother believed or his childhood church taught or even what he wanted to be true but instead on what the Bible says. In the deconstruction, Yancey got rid of the toxic mold and in the reconstruction found *his* beliefs, *his* faith, and *his* relationship with Jesus. He discovered a new faith he could wholly embrace; a faith that was personal, credible, and beautiful.

We could say that, for Philip Yancey, deconstruction was a form of discipleship.

In the Christian context, a disciple is someone who believes in Jesus, has chosen to follow him, and becomes more and more like him. Discipleship is spiritual growth that leads to transformation into Christlikeness. Ideally, someone is discipled by another believer. But I wonder whether perhaps a Christian can also be discipled by the journey through doubt, the journey from a healthy deconstruction into a biblical reconstruction.

Deconstruction is a dismantling, a tearing down, but to be healthy it's also necessary for a building up to take place.

So how do you rebuild your faith?

When there are all kinds of people pointing you to their understanding of God, whom do you listen to? They're not all the same. Some say God is full of wrath and ready to judge. Others claim God is compassionate and ready to cuddle. Is God the God of the Baptists or Catholics or charismatics? All kinds of people are pointing you to their understanding of God. So who do you listen to?

None of them.

You look at Jesus.

As he told us in Matthew 7, you let his words, his example, and his truth rebuild your faith.

One time Jesus was talking to people who wanted to know what God as the Father in heaven is really like. Jesus told them, "'If you had really known me, you would know who my Father is. From now on, you do know him and have seen him!' Philip said, 'Lord, show us the Father, and we will be satisfied.' Jesus replied, 'Have I been with you all this time, Philip, and yet you still don't know who I am? Anyone who has seen me has seen the Father!'" (John 14:7–9 NLT).

Jesus was telling them that he is our picture of God. If we see him and get to know him, we have seen and gotten to know God. He was declaring that our understanding of God should be centered on him.

The more we know Jesus, the more we know God himself. And the Bible gives us a very detailed picture of Jesus, which allows us to develop a very accurate picture of God. Being convinced that God looks like Jesus is what can help us get through our confusion and rebuild a faith that is true, a faith we can base our beliefs upon.

When you look at the life of Jesus, you realize he was amazing in his character, his love, his compassion. The way he cared for those who were hurting and cried with his friends. The way he treated people with grace and tenderness. The way he saw the best in the worst of sinners and reached out to the lonely, the lost, and the least of these. If God is like that, I can trust him, no matter what's going on in my life.

And God is exactly like that.

You rebuild your faith starting with Jesus.

And then you rebuild your beliefs based on the Bible.

How do you do that?

I would encourage you to come to the Bible prayerfully, with the most sincere, objective view you can muster, and to always read Scripture through the lens of Jesus and his love.

It's like when you're doing a jigsaw puzzle and you look at all the pieces and feel confused. What do you do? You look at the picture on the box. The picture helps you make sense of each individual piece and how they all fit together. Jesus is the picture on the box. We interpret and understand everything in the Bible through him.

It may be scary to go through a thoughtful deconstruction, but it's worth it. You will grow as the result of change, but change isn't always conformable. Don't give up. Don't settle for deconstruction only. Your story, your faith, ends not in death but in resurrection. Keep moving forward, knowing that new life is coming on the other side as you reconstruct.

New Life

I want to take you back to the lake Peter was walking on, then found himself sinking in.

Remember when Jesus asked him, "Why did you doubt?"

I'm curious—do you read that question as an accusation or an invitation?

I wouldn't be surprised if you've thought of it as a disappointed accusation, like "Why did you doubt, you loser?" But knowing what we do about Jesus, that he *is* love, full of grace, and consistently compassionate, maybe we've been reading that question the wrong way.

What if this question is not an accusation but an invitation?

What if Jesus wasn't shaming Peter—which is not something Jesus seems to do—but inviting him into a deeper faith?

Did you notice what Jesus did when he asked Peter the question? He reached out his hand to help. That's what love does.

It seems as though Jesus was asking, "Peter, why are you doubting? You know me. Remember the water and wine? The loaves and fishes? The blind eyes that now see? The deaf ears that now hear? You know all of this,

Peter. You know *me*. That's why you got out of the boat. You have great faith. So why are you doubting? Let's get you out of the water and back onto the boat."

I want to encourage you that if you start to doubt, if wind and waves are tripping up your faith journey, don't panic. See doubt as Jesus' invitation into a more examined, more thoughtful, deeper faith.

> SEE DOUBT AS JESUS' INVITATION INTO A MORE EXAMINED, MORE THOUGHTFUL, DEEPER FAITH.

Later, Peter would have another bout with doubt. After Jesus was arrested and as he was put on trial, the night before he was crucified, Peter denied Jesus three times. I read one commentator who claimed Peter deconverted that night. His argument was based on the fact that Peter denied his faith in Jesus as the Son of God three times.

I don't think that was a deconversion, but it was certainly a moment of profound doubt.

What I do know is what Jesus did in response. Peter doubted, to the extent that he denied Jesus, and Jesus responded by reaching out to Peter.

After his resurrection, Jesus met with Peter on a beach. Three times Peter had denied Jesus, and three times Jesus asked, "Do you love me?" Each time, when Peter said yes, Jesus told him, "Feed my sheep" (John 21:14–17).

What was Jesus doing? He was forgiving Peter's sins and rebuilding Peter's broken faith. Peter had been the sheep who wandered away. Jesus had lovingly pursued him, found him on a beach, and was bringing him back into the fold, exactly what he taught about himself as the Shepherd in Matthew 18.

Jesus was resurrected, living a new life, and he was now inviting Peter into new life with a reconstructed faith.

By saying "Feed my sheep," Jesus was also restoring Peter to his place in ministry. Who did God choose to preach at Pentecost, the "grand opening" of his church? The day three thousand people were saved? Peter, whose faith was built *after* doubt, who experienced an amazing life—with God—life after deconstruction, life after reconstruction, life after doubt.

Because doubt is not the enemy of faith but an invitation into a deeper faith.

About thirty years after he was forgiven by Jesus, Peter wrote from personal experience, "For 'you were like sheep going astray,' but now you have returned to the Shepherd and Overseer of your souls" (1 Peter 2:25). Who better to say that than a lost sheep who was rescued by the reaching hand of Jesus in the middle of his doubts?

If you're doubting, Jesus is reaching out to you.

He is love.

He loves you, and he is a Good Shepherd who will, in love, come after you when you're lost, to bring you home to his love.

That's how good he is.

That's why I follow him.

And my hope is that when you are facing your doubts, you will deconstruct, then *reconstruct* a faith in him that is personal, credible, and beautiful.

> **What, then, shall we say in response to these things? If God is for us, who can be against us? He who did not spare his own Son, but gave him up for us all—how will he not also, along with him, graciously give us all things? . . . Christ Jesus who died—more than that, who was raised to life—is at the right hand of God and is also interceding for us. Who shall separate us from the love of Christ?**
>
> **—ROMANS 8:31-32, 34-35**

CHAPTER 2 EXERCISE

1. Were you previously aware of or have you had personal experience with deconstruction? Explain. If your answer is no, what are your thoughts after being introduced to the subject?

2. How would you describe the construction of your faith? Talk about your "faith house."

3. What has been the biggest crack in your faith foundation? What faulty beliefs have you had to face or now feel you need to address?

4. What is your view on how Jesus encouraged people to deconstruct and reconstruct their faith, as he did for Peter and the Jewish people in their expectations about the Messiah?

5. Do you think that you have any biblically inaccurate beliefs or biased filters on Scripture? Explain.

6. Why do you suppose when so many people start to doubt and struggle with faith, they will "tear the house down" rather than do the work of separating lies from truth?

7. What are your thoughts on this statement: "Without a death there can be no resurrection"? How might this truth apply to your own faith journey?

8. As a disciple of Jesus, why would it be important to separate what is true in your beliefs from what is not true?

9. After reading this chapter, is there any aspect of your faith that you sense might need to be deconstructed and reconstructed? Explain.

10. How does the story of Jesus' response to Peter encourage you in the places of doubt and faith in your life?

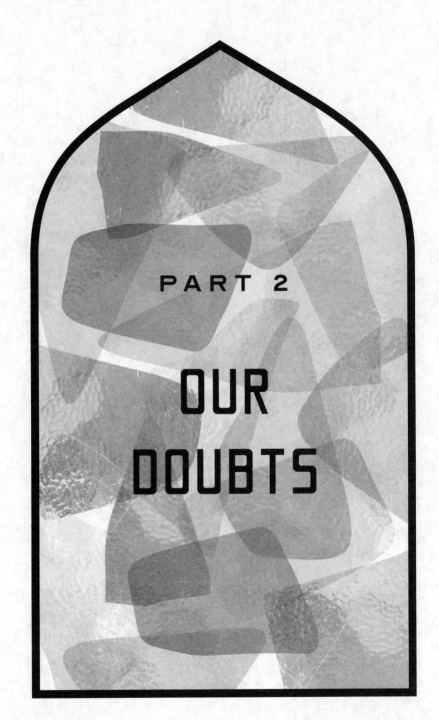

PART 2

OUR
DOUBTS

CHAPTER 3

Why Should I Believe God Is Good?

Sarah is one of the sweetest, godliest, and most encouraging Christians you could ever meet. If you had one conversation with her, you'd want to be her friend and would sense her genuine relationship with Jesus and love for God.

But if you heard her story, you'd be shocked by her pain.

Her talented and vibrant eighth-grade son, Caleb, was killed in a tragic accident. He was only thirteen years old.

The loss of Caleb crushed Sarah and felt like too much to bear.

Yet when it seemed as though things couldn't possibly get worse, sadly, they did. Much worse.

Sarah's husband, Jim, was a good husband and dad who had battled chronic depression for decades. He had changed careers and started studying to become a pastor. The family felt optimistic as his outlook on life got better and he made progress in healing from the despair that had haunted him for so long. But when Caleb died, so did Jim's hope.

Shortly after losing her son to an accident, Sarah lost her husband to suicide.

She cried out to God in debilitating anguish, "Why, God? Why would you let this happen to me? Why would you let this happen to my family?"

In Christian circles we like to say, "God is good! All the time!" Yet when he appears to reward faithful service with the loss of a son and a husband, well, that's where many folks might throw his goodness into question.

Maybe something tragic has happened in your life that causes you to relate to Sarah's pain, such as one or more of these:

- You lost a loved one.
- You lost your job.
- Your parents split up or your spouse asked for a divorce.
- You trusted someone and they grossly abused that trust.
- You battle depression, anxiety, a chronic disease, or migraines.
- You are tortured by temptations that feel overwhelming.
- You look around at the world and see the innocent suffering, such as children being killed in mass school shootings.

So . . . God is good?

All the time?

Is that just a bumper-sticker slogan for the blissfully ignorant or reality for those who follow Jesus?

Why Did God Let It Happen?

John Goldingay was a pastor and seminary professor. He preached that God is loving, God is good, God is trustworthy. John spent his life faithfully serving his congregation, students, and beloved wife, Ann. Then one day, out of nowhere, Ann started having odd muscle spasms. She began struggling to keep her balance, which quickly became concerning. A visit to the doctor and some tests confirmed their worst fears. Ann had multiple sclerosis. Soon she struggled to move her arms and legs. Walking went from difficult to impossible. Ann's condition continued to worsen until she finally passed away. She and John had been married for forty-three years.

Once again, as in Sarah's situation, the question is, "Why?"

If you've ever doubted God because of something that seems unfair, you're certainly not alone. People have been questioning God's goodness, based on what happens in this world, for a long, long time.

Three hundred years before the birth of Jesus, a Greek philosopher named Epicurus made a three-point argument denying the goodness of God.

1. If God is not *able* to prevent evil, if he can't stop bad things from happening, then God must not be all powerful.
2. If God is not *willing* to prevent evil, then he must not be all good.
3. If God is both willing and able to prevent evil from happening, then why does evil exist?[1]

As followers of Jesus, do we have an answer to that question?

Are we forced to concede that God is either unable or unwilling to prevent evil?

Or are evil and suffering actually *not* contrary to the existence of an all-powerful, all-good God? Or to the story of the Bible? Is it possible that Christianity

1. Makes sense of the existence of good and evil?
2. Gives meaning to the existence of good and evil?
3. Offers a solution for the evil and suffering we experience?

God's Book

Some might assume that God's Word—the Bible—is only a book of answers. But it's interesting that Scripture is also full of questions. Instead of ignoring the

IS IT POSSIBLE THAT CHRISTIANITY ACTUALLY OFFERS A SOLUTION FOR THE EVIL AND SUFFERING WE EXPERIENCE?

negative aspects of life (because it doesn't necessarily always make God look good), it tells countless stories of heartbreak, confusion, suffering, and pain.

The longest book in the Bible consists of 150 psalms, which are prayers and songs written by people to God and about God. Some have themes of praise and gratitude. But many ask questions:

- "Why, God?"
- "How long, God?"
- "Where are you, God?"

Exactly the kind of questions we have today.

In Acts 13:22, God describes David as "a man after my own heart" because he so loves and trusts God that he cries out to him in the Psalms:

- "Why, LORD, do you stand far off? Why do you hide yourself in times of trouble?" (10:1).
- "Why are you so far from saving me, so far from my cries of anguish? My God, I cry out by day, but you do not answer, by night, but I find no rest" (22:1–2).
- "Will the Lord reject forever? Will he never show his favor again? Has his unfailing love vanished forever? Has his promise failed for all time?" (77:7–8).

Psalm 77, from which that last passage was taken, and eleven other psalms are attributed to a man named Asaph, who was the worship leader of the tabernacle choir. In Psalm 73 he complains about the success and good fortune of those who deny God. He writes, "For I envied the arrogant when I saw the prosperity of the wicked. They have no struggles; their bodies are healthy and strong. They are free from common human burdens; they are not plagued by human ills" (Ps. 73:3–5).

He goes on to describe how these prideful people have the best abs and most Instagram followers and always somehow manage to get the new Jordans when they come out. (Okay, so that's my modern-day paraphrase, but I'm sure you already figured that out.) Asaph sadly concludes, "Surely in vain I have kept my heart pure and have washed my hands in innocence. All day long I have been afflicted, and every morning brings new punishments" (Ps. 73:13–14).

If you've ever doubted God's goodness because of some injustice, tragedy, or crushing disappointment, as you can see, you're not alone. Even God's worship leader Asaph cried out, "Where is God? Why would he let things go down like this? It just doesn't seem fair."

David and Asaph weren't the only ones who questioned God. So did Jeremiah, who became known as "the weeping prophet." He wrote a book of the Old Testament called Lamentations. The original translation of the name of this book is "How?" The book is a prayerful lament born of Jeremiah's sadness. Here's an example of his pain: "I am the man who has seen affliction by the rod of the LORD's wrath. He has driven me away and made me walk in darkness rather than light; indeed, he has turned his hand against me again and again, all day long" (Lam. 3:1–3).

In the New Testament, John the Baptist, the man whose sole purpose was to prepare the way for Jesus, was wrongly arrested and sat in prison awaiting execution. Surely Jesus could have rescued his friend. But he didn't, and John was beheaded.

In Hebrews 11, the passage known as the Faith Hall of Fame, we find some disturbing verses that don't exactly help in recruiting new members for the early church: "Some faced jeers and flogging, and even chains and imprisonment. They were put to death by stoning; they were sawed in two; they were killed by the sword. They went about in sheepskins and goatskins, destitute, persecuted and mistreated—the world was not worthy of them. They wandered in deserts and mountains, living in caves and in holes in the ground" (vv. 36–38).

God's book does not protect his own image by censoring any talk of evil or suffering. Instead, the Bible seems to highlight it.

Even Jesus, the Son of God, though a conquering, victorious King, is called "a Man of sorrows and acquainted with grief" (Isa. 53:3 NKJV).

Why would God show us so many of his chosen ones, his faithful servants, complaining about him and questioning his goodness?

Perhaps we're supposed to learn that God can be loving *and* allow suffering at the same time. Let's try to understand why.

If Love Is a Choice, Suffering Is a Possibility

Our question is this: If God is a loving God, why would he allow suffering?

The answer is God allows suffering *because* he is a loving God.

Let's try to understand this by carefully walking through some weighty ideas.

For starters, who is God? While the world tells us that love is an emotion, Scripture teaches us above all else that God is love (1 John 4:16). Love isn't just what God does. Love is who God is. God *is* love, and he created us for love, to be loved by him and to love him, and to be loved by other people and to love them (Matt. 22:37–39).

That is awesome.

And that is the problem.

Why?

Because for love to be love, it must also be a choice. We know that, right? Imagine someone you don't love demanding that you love them, threatening, "Love me now or else!" Would you love that person? No. Because you can't be forced to love. Love is love only when it's freely chosen.

You know who came up with that concept? God.

At his core, God is love, and he made us for love, which necessitated his creating us with free will, along with the power to choose.

That's the issue.

- If you have the ability to choose love, you also have the ability to choose hate.
- If you can choose what's right, you can also choose what's wrong.
- If you can choose what's good, you can also choose what's evil.

If we didn't have the power to choose, we could never freely choose to love. But it's also our freedom to choose that brought sin into the world. People, starting with the first (that's Adam and Eve) and continuing through to the one who wrote this book (that's me) and the one who is reading this book (that's you), have used free will to choose to sin. And, ultimately, it's sin that leads to the evil and suffering in the world.

> GOD IS LOVE, WHICH NECESSITATED HIS CREATING US WITH FREE WILL, ALONG WITH THE POWER TO CHOOSE.

So could God remove evil and suffering?

Well, sure.

But to do so he'd have to remove our freedom to choose, and thereby remove love.

Or he would have to remove us.

If There Is No God, Who Decides There's Evil?

People wonder, "Why is there evil if there is a God?" and some argue, "Because there's evil, I don't believe there is a God." But perhaps the question they should be asking is, "If there is no God, how can we say there is evil?"

And if there's no God, who decides what's evil? Who is the judge? Who creates the standard for what's good and what's not?

For example, I have a little sister, Lisa, who is three years younger than I am. I love Lisa more than I can describe and will defend her until the day I die. But growing up, like any normal older brother, I picked on her—all the time.

Whenever I did, at some point she would reach her limit and yell, "Stop it!" She would continue with a tirade of words that rhymed with "Stop it." She'd yell, "Stop it! Cop it! Pop it! Lop it! Whop it!" I'd laugh at her lack of rage-fueled creativity, and she would respond with two dreaded words: "I'm telling!" She would run out of the room, but I'd race past to trump her "I'm telling" with my very own "No, *I'm* telling!" I assumed if I was the first to explain the situation and present my side, I'd get closer to a fair trial and possibly even be declared not guilty.

Question: What if my sister and I had no parents? Without a mom or dad, who would have decided who was wrong or right?

I would have believed I was right and Lisa was wrong.

Lisa would have believed she was right and I was wrong.

Without an authority to turn to, we would have been left to our own opinions with no objective standard of right or wrong.

So what if there is no God? There would be no moral point of reference and no way of calling anything universally wrong or right.

If there is no God, if it's all just Darwinian evolution and survival of the fittest, why is one person's opinion better than another's? If someone can overpower a weaker person in some way, isn't that just the way the whole system works? But almost no one believes that. We'd say it's wrong. Why? Because there *is* a God, and he has put in us all an innate sense of right and wrong (Rom. 2:15).

So what does all of this mean? The presence of evil and suffering isn't proof that God does not exist. If we look at this issue with intellectual integrity, we need to admit that our belief in evil and suffering is actually proof that God does exist.

The Presence of Suffering Doesn't Mean the Absence of Love

Let's go back to Sarah, the sweet Christian woman who lost both her son and husband. You can only imagine her questions and doubts as she grieved her profound losses. After all, she'd been faithful to God. Her son didn't do anything wrong. Her husband was making progress overcoming his depression. Like so many others, she was tempted to believe, *If God allows suffering like mine, then he can't be a loving God.* Some might even say, "If you suffer, that must mean God doesn't love you. If he did, why would he allow it?"

In the middle of real grief, deep pain, serious betrayal, or tragic loss, it's easy to believe the presence of suffering is evidence of an absence of love.

That's simply not true.

We know it's not true because we see it every day.

In the summer of 2020, I had surgery. The doctor (who is also a friend) didn't hate me, but he made me suffer through the surgery. And I hurt after the surgery. He brought me pain. Not because he didn't love me but because of the promise of something better.

I have another good friend who is a physical therapist. He sometimes causes me pain. He stretches me and works on my painful spots. Before he begins, he'll even warn me, "This is going to hurt." Does he make me suffer because he doesn't love me? No. He does it because of the promise of something better.

If you go to a therapist, she may ask questions that take you to difficult memories from childhood. That. Is. Not. Fun. Are therapists cruel? No. They care and believe it's the path to healing. They're leading you to something better.

Have you ever seen someone's arm dislocated? That's some intense pain. But what makes it even worse is when the arm has to be popped back into the socket. Whoever relocates the bone has to create hurt to heal. What happens afterward? Incredible relief because the arm is realigned correctly. Again, leading to something better.

The same is true with parents who discipline their children. Good parents don't discipline children to be mean or cruel. Good parents correct their children because they love them.

In healthy relationships, we've come to understand that "tough love" is not abuse but simply necessary correction to persuade someone to take responsibility for his or her actions. With God's love we have to remember the presence of pain does not indicate an absence of love. In fact, oftentimes, the presence of real pain is the evidence of real love.

Why Do Bad Things Happen to Good People?

I was in the bleachers watching my son Stephen play soccer, seated next to another dad. We started a casual conversation, mostly commenting on the game. Then, after a few minutes, I noticed he was looking as if he might recognize me. He asked, "By any chance, are you the pastor of a church?" I nodded yes. He said, "I thought so." After introducing himself as Bruce, he paused, seemed to swallow hard, and asked in an incredibly sincere way, "I'm just curious. How do you believe in a God when he doesn't even care?" There was no edge or accusation. I could sense his pain. He was genuinely asking a hard question.

"If you are comfortable, please tell me why you're asking that," I said quietly, out of respect for our being in earshot of other parents.

Without hesitation, for the next several minutes his hurt poured out. He told me he grew up in a Catholic church and always went to Mass. He married a Catholic girl in the church and they always went to Mass. They had a son and wanted a daughter. Got pregnant again. Another son; still wanted a daughter. Got pregnant again. This time God answered their prayers—they had a daughter! Unfortunately, she had a severe heart issue and needed to go in for a high-risk surgery. They prayed, their priest prayed, they lit candles and prayed some more. But their daughter died in surgery.

As he shared those words, my heart sank. While my healthy son continued to run around on the soccer field, I wondered how to best answer his pain-soaked question, "How do you believe in a God when he doesn't even care?"

Hurting for him, I prayed a silent prayer asking God to give me wisdom in how to respond. Yet before I had a chance to speak, Bruce continued. Fighting back tears, he pled his case, "I'm a good person. I always tried to do what's right. I always believed in God. Why did he allow this to happen to me? Why? Why do bad things happen to good people?"

It's a difficult question, not because there isn't a good answer, but because no one wants to hear the good answer. And I definitely didn't want to give this answer to Bruce in this moment in the middle of his pain. For hurting people, timing is everything.

But there is an answer.

Do *you* want to hear the good answer?

Okay, here it is, but I warn you, you won't like it.

Why do bad things happen to good people?

They don't, because we're *not* good people.

I told you that you wouldn't like it. But it's true.

That's what God tells us in the Bible, consistently.

Just like my new friend at the soccer game, I know what you're thinking: *I may not be perfect, but I have a good heart.* Most folks believe themselves to be "a good person." But, unfortunately, that's simply not true for any of us. Here's God's diagnosis: "The heart is deceitful above all things and beyond cure. Who can understand it?" (Jer. 17:9). While I can't always understand my own heart, I can say that I know I don't have a good heart. Why? My heart has led me to think bad thoughts, do sinful things, and say hurtful words.

"Why do bad things happen to good people?" is an impossible question to answer, because none of us are good people.

The truth is that "all have sinned and fall short of the glory of God" (Rom. 3:23) and "there is no one righteous, not even one" (Rom. 3:10). Without the renewing work of Christ, none of us have good hearts.

> **WITHOUT THE RENEWING WORK OF CHRIST, NONE OF US HAVE GOOD HEARTS.**

In Mark 10, there's an interesting conversation where Jesus focuses on what is called good. As Jesus was starting out on his way to Jerusalem, a man came running up to him, fell down on his knees, and asked, "Good Teacher, what must I do to inherit eternal life?"

"Why do you call me good?" Jesus asked. "Only God is truly good."

After a brief discussion about the commandments and the man saying he had kept all the ones Jesus mentioned, things took an interesting turn. "Looking at the man, Jesus felt genuine love for him. 'There is still one thing you haven't done,' he told him. 'Go and sell all your possessions and give the money to the poor, and you will have treasure in heaven. Then come, follow me.' At this the man's face fell, and he went away sad, for he had many possessions" (vv. 21–22 NLT).

So, actually, we *can* answer the question. There has been one good person. Jesus. And something really bad happened to him. In fact, he volunteered for the pain and suffering. The one good person, who had never done anything wrong, took the punishment for all our sin.

Jesus, the sinless Son of God, gave up the glory of heaven and was born into poverty. Later, when he grew in popularity, his family thought he had lost his mind. Even later he was abandoned by his friends. He was falsely accused. Wrongly imprisoned. Beaten. Tortured. Stripped naked. Hung shamefully on a cross. Then the only one who was good, the only one who had never sinned became sin for us. He was separated from his Father so we wouldn't have to be separated from him anymore. Jesus gave up his life so he could give us life.

God allowed his only Son to go through all of that suffering and pain. Why?

Why did God allow that bad thing to happen to the one good person?

Love. Because "God so loved the world that he gave his one and only Son" (John 3:16).

Why does God allow bad things to happen in our lives?

I don't know what the answer is in every specific situation, but I know what the answer is not.

The answer is not that God doesn't love you.

God loves you so much he sent Jesus to die for you—and it wasn't because you're good; it's because he is love.

> Christ died for us at a time when we were helpless and sinful. No one is really willing to die for an honest person, though someone might be willing to die for a truly good person. But God showed how much he loved us by having Christ die for us, even though we were sinful.
>
> But there is more! Now that God has accepted us because Christ sacrificed his life's blood, we will also be kept safe from God's anger.
>
> **—ROMANS 5:6-9 CEV**

God loves you so much he allowed the worst possible thing to happen to his own Son when you were at your worst. You can be absolutely certain that anything bad that happens to you is not because God doesn't love you.

So that's what the answer is not, but what is the answer? Why does God allow bad things to happen?

Again, I don't know.

At the beginning of the chapter, I mentioned John Goldingay. In his book *The Jesus Creed*, author Scot McKnight shares John's words describing his wife's losing battle with multiple sclerosis. John says, "All of us search for meaning in tragedy and any inadequate answer to the problem of suffering is preferable to the honest and true answer, 'We do not know,' which is why people go around repeating inadequate answers." John goes on to say, "There may sometimes be explanations for calamity that we do not know. But we have to live with God without knowing them."[2]

And then there's Sarah, who faced life without her son and husband. Why did she have to endure those losses? While I can't know for sure, Sarah gave me her permission to share an email she sent me that touched my heart. After I had preached a message on seeking healing in depression, she wrote, "It's with tears in my eyes and a heart of overflowing thankfulness that I write to you. I was wondering in your sermon today how your words may have spoken to my husband. Your message of truth encourages me and fills me with hope for all those who heard it. May God richly bless your every effort to reach those stuck in the miry pit and bless those who are willing to get muddy and desire to help pull the broken and hurting out."

Then this precious woman, who had lost not one but two men, signed her email:

> Jesus is enough.
>
> —Sarah

Jesus is enough.

Today, Sarah leads a group for those who are recovering from trauma and seeking healing from tragic loss.

Is it possible that Christianity actually makes sense of, gives meaning to, and offers a solution for the evil and suffering we experience?

We don't know why, but we know we can trust God. We can live with God without knowing the answers because he is love and he loved us enough to send Jesus to die for us.

And I think Jesus' death might help us understand at least part of the reason why.

Jesus died, but he didn't stay dead. Why did God allow the worst possible outcome to happen?

Because he loves you.

Because God knew something better was coming. Today, we may know this:

- There can be victory after loss.
- There can be healing after hurt.
- There can be freedom after bondage.
- There can be resurrection after death.

GOD NEVER PROMISED TO PROTECT US FROM PAIN. HOWEVER, HE DID PROMISE HIS PRESENCE IN THE MIDST OF OUR PAIN.

God never promised to protect us from pain. In fact, Jesus assured us of the opposite, saying, "In this world you will have trouble" (John 16:33).

However, he did promise his presence in the midst of our pain. If you are hurt, depressed, or discouraged, hold on to these promises from God's Word:

- "God is our refuge and strength, an ever-present help in trouble" (Ps. 46:1).
- "The LORD is near to all who call on him, to all who call on him in truth. He fulfills the desires of those who fear him; he hears their cry and saves them" (Ps. 145:18–19).
- "God has said, 'Never will I leave you; never will I forsake you.' So

we say with confidence, "The Lord is my helper; I will not be afraid" (Heb. 13:5–6).

- Jesus said, "Now is your time of grief, but I will see you again and you will rejoice, and no one will take away your joy" (John 16:22).

He promised something better is coming.

Just like Jesus, we will suffer.

Just like Jesus, we will die.

Just like Jesus, we will *rise*.

Goldingay explains how in the face of tragedy we want answers but don't know the answers. He then encourages us to walk on, in faith and in pain. He says, "We are invited to name our hopelessness and to let ourselves be soaked, enfolded, immersed in the counter-story of Jesus' life, death, and resurrection, because they are the basis for hope."[3]

We have hope in this life because we know there's life after this life.

Something better is coming.

Check out how the Bible describes the life after this life: "Look! God's dwelling place is now among the people, and he will dwell with them. They will be his people, and God himself will be with them and be their God. 'He will wipe every tear from their eyes. There will be no more death' or mourning or crying or pain, for the old order of things has passed away. He who was seated on the throne said, 'I am making everything new!'" (Rev. 21:3–5).

Even in our doubts, questions, and suffering, we can have hope because something better is coming.

One day when we are united with Jesus, there will be no more tears or death or mourning or crying or pain. No more sickness or rejection or heartache. No more shame or grief or depression. No more abuse. No more crying yourself to sleep.

Something better is coming.

But we're not there yet.

We still live in a sin-infested world where, because love is possible, so is evil.

That might cause some to doubt.

That might lead us to ask hard questions.

That might lead us to hard answers.

I think of a sweet little girl Amy and I know and love. Her dad sexually abused her repeatedly. She finds it almost impossible to trust anyone. She asked me why this happened to her.

I think of an amazing family whose new home had a gas leak and exploded. Their youngest daughter was killed. They understandably ask why.

And of a thirty-one-year-old mom of two who passed away. I met with her husband. He just wanted to know why.

I can't really answer their questions. The best I can do is cry with them.

When you're in the middle of something that seems unfair, it can be easy to conclude that God must not be good. But we know that's not true. So we don't run from him. Instead, we grab hold and we don't let go.

Remember Asaph, the worship leader of the temple choir? The guy who complained about the prosperity and abs and Instagram followers of the wicked and thought, "Surely in vain I have kept my heart pure." After pouring out his complaint to God, he took a deep breath and remembered what he knew to be true.

> Yet I am always with you;
> you hold me by my right hand.
> You guide me with your counsel,
> and afterward you will take me into glory.
>
> —PSALM 73:23–24

God's presence was with him even in his pain.

God had something better coming.

So if you're living in pain and you're wondering where God is, remember you're living in the not-there-yet. The good news is that by the grace, the power, the glory, and the goodness of God something better is coming. God is good.

And God is with you.

He hurts with you.

For now, grab hold of him and don't let go.

Someday you can look back and realize that God was good, all the time.

My prayer is that you will experience the reality of what Sarah found in the midst of her loss and pain: Jesus is enough.

> Let us draw near to God with a sincere heart and with the full assurance that faith brings. . . . Let us hold unswervingly to the hope we profess, for he who promised is faithful.
> —HEBREWS 10:22-23

CHAPTER 3 EXERCISE

1. What has been your most challenging tragedy in life that created tough questions for your faith? Explain.
2. In response to Epicurus' argument, how do you explain that God can be both all powerful and all good in the midst of our pain and suffering?
3. Consider the book of Lamentations and Asaph's psalms. Why do you suppose God has allowed prayers of doubt, questions, and lamentations to be included in his Word?
4. Think back to the "If Love Is a Choice, Suffering Is a Possibility" section. What are your thoughts on the relationship between free will, love, and sin?
5. How is our innate sense of right and wrong evidence for the existence of God?
6. Do you agree that sometimes "the presence of real pain is the evidence of real love"? Why or why not?
7. Why do you think that the biblical truth "No one is acceptable to God" (Rom. 3:10 CEV) can be difficult for people to accept?
8. How do you feel about Sarah's response to her incredible loss, saying, "Jesus is enough"? Do you relate to this or reject it? Explain.
9. How can the gospel—the hope provided through Jesus' death and resurrection—change how we view the suffering and pain in our lives?
10. After reading this chapter, do you feel you have a better understanding of the possible answers to the universal question "Why, God?" Explain.

CHAPTER 4

Why Doesn't God Answer My Prayers?

I held my wife, Amy, as she sobbed and sobbed. Her brother, David, was only thirty-four years old when he died.

"We trusted God and now David is gone. I just don't get it. We claimed God's promises. We had unwavering faith. We did everything we were supposed to do. Why didn't God heal him? Why didn't he answer our prayers?"

I empathized with her pain. I'm guessing you might too.

In circumstances like this, prayer can be very confusing.

That's not how you expect a pastor to open a chapter on prayer in a book about growing past your doubts, is it? But let's be honest. It is confusing, right?

I'll explain. Stick with me.

If I asked, "Do you believe in the power of prayer?" it's likely you'd say you do.

It's hard not to.

I mean, if you read the Bible, you see it all over.

Joshua, the prophet, prayed for the sun to stand still, and it did! For an entire "this is going to absolutely put daylight saving time to shame" day (Josh. 10:12–14).

And what about the time Elijah faced off against hundreds of prophets of a false god called Baal and he needed a sacrifice to catch on fire to prove his was the true God? So he drenched the altar with water. (My rudimentary science background tells me the elements needed for fire are oxygen, heat, and fuel, and that H_2O is *extremely* counterproductive.) Then Elijah prayed and—inferno! Adele's singing "Set Fire to the Rain," Elijah's yelling, "Who's your daddy?!" and the prophets of Baal are history (1 Kings 18:22–40).

Then there's Daniel, who wouldn't stop praying even when King Darius made it illegal to pray. The king's response was to throw Daniel into a den of hungry lions. Daniel's response to the king was to keep praying. And God's response? He shut the mouths of the lions (Dan. 6:6–23).

God is good all the time, and all the time God is good.

Do you believe God answers prayer?

It's hard not to.

My faith in God to answer prayers isn't just because of what I see in Scripture but also because of what I experience in my life. Over the years, I've seen God do wild, inexplicable things in response to prayers I've prayed.

I saw a lady's failing eyesight healed.

I listened to doctors who were baffled by the disappearance of a cancer.

I saw a guy who had smoked for fourteen years quit after we prayed.

I even watched a devil worshiper physically change when someone prayed for him. And then the devil worshiper became a disciple of Jesus!

I'm hoping you have a few answered-prayer stories of your own. Maybe God provided for you when you asked him to meet a need.

Or he gave you wisdom when you asked.

Perhaps God helped you overcome an addiction.

Or he comforted you when you were hurting while you prayed and worshiped.

So do you believe God answers prayers?

It's hard not to.

But in light of any unanswered prayers, it can be confusing.

Do I believe God answers prayers? Yes. But some times are more difficult than others. If I'm being honest, sometimes it's really difficult.

Contrary to the "answered prayer list" I just gave you, God has also *not* granted many of the requests I've made of him. Sometimes it has felt as though he has ignored many of my prayers over the years.

Amy and I had some close friends who confided in us that they were struggling as a couple. Day after day, we prayed faith-filled prayers for their marriage. They got divorced.

My pastor Nick, the person who had the most impact on my spiritual formation and call to ministry, got COVID. Most people recovered from COVID. Still, I wasn't taking any chances. I prayed. Nick's condition worsened. I gathered our best prayer warriors from the church. We prayed intense, bold, devil-crushing, heaven-shaking prayers. Nick died.

Then there was the time I was invited to pray before a football game at a Christian school. What do you pray when both teams are from Christian schools? Not for one team to win—that's biased, and you may meet up with some parents from the other team after the game. So I prayed for safety and good sportsmanship. How did God answer that prayer? A kid snapped an opposing player's leg in two, causing a massive bench-clearing fight to break out, and they canceled the game. (It's no wonder they never asked me to pray again!)

So do I believe God answers prayer?

Sometimes it's hard to.

It's confusing.

You'd think the Bible would help make prayer less confusing. But sometimes it doesn't. Like what about the promise Jesus makes in John 14:13–14: "And I will do whatever you ask in my name, so that the Father may be glorified in the Son. You may ask me for anything in my name, and I will do it."

All of those times I prayed and God answered my prayers, I always asked in Jesus' name.

And those times God didn't do what I asked, I also prayed all of those prayers in Jesus' name.

I understand why the Anglican theologian and intellectual giant C. S. Lewis had doubts. After years of God faithfully answering his prayers, he asked that his wife would be healed of bone cancer. But God did not heal her, and she died. You can feel the tension ripping apart Lewis' heart when he wrote after she died,

Go to him when your need is desperate, when all other help is vain, and what do you find? A door slammed in your face, and a sound of bolting and double bolting on the inside. After that, silence. You may as well turn away. The longer you wait, the more emphatic the silence will become. There are no lights in the windows. It might be an empty house. Was it ever inhabited? It seemed so once. And that seeming was as strong as this. What can this mean? Why is He so present a commander in our time of prosperity and so very absent a help in time of trouble?[1]

God is good all the time, and sometimes he doesn't do what we think he should.

Prayer is powerful. And confusing.

God responds to it! And sometimes he doesn't!

Prayer is dynamic. And disappointing.

Prayer leads us into God's blessing.

But it can also lead us to become bitter.

If you prayed and believed God would answer, but he didn't do what you requested, the letdown might have birthed spiritual discouragement that has grown into intense spiritual doubts. You likely have questions. You might wonder:

- Is the issue with God or me?
- Am I praying wrong?
- Do I even understand what prayer is?
- Does God care?

Let's see if we can answer these questions, clear up some confusion, and maybe even stamp out our doubts.

The Purpose of Prayer

There was a movie some years ago in which the egotistical main character says he feels as though life is a movie and he is the star. Everyone else in the world—the cashier at the grocery store, his parents, the women he dates, his neighbors—were all just supporting actors who made cameo appearances in the movie, which was really all about his life.

Sound crazy?

What's crazier is that I'm tempted to think that way too.

I assume you're the same.

The belief that the world revolves around us reveals humanity's foundational issue at the very heart of sin.

This may be hard to hear because we've all been conditioned by our self-centered nature, as well as our self-absorbed culture, but you are not the main character in the story. To be clear: you are not even the main character in your own story.

Sorry to be blunt, but someone had to say it.

Who is the real main character?

God.

He is the star of the story. He should be the star of *your* story.

So what does this have to do with prayer?

When we think we're the main character, it's natural to believe that God exists to serve us. If someone listened in on all your prayers, I wonder if they'd conclude you believe that God is your divine assistant who exists to make your life better.

But it's not about you.

And it's not about me.

Even though I know spiritually that life is about God's glory, God's will, and God's plan, not my own, my prayers don't always reflect that truth. When I'm honest about many of my prayers, I have to admit that a lot of my praying is an attempt to control God. I tell him what I want, what is best, and what he needs to do. But that's not the purpose of prayer.

We need to embrace the reality that God is the star of the story. He does not exist to serve us. We exist to serve him. This truth is displayed in the life of Jesus throughout the Gospels.

When we come to terms with that, we understand that the purpose of prayer is not to get God to do our will. The purpose of prayer is to know God so we can do his will.

> THE PURPOSE OF PRAYER IS NOT TO GET GOD TO DO OUR WILL BUT TO KNOW HIM SO WE CAN DO HIS WILL.

The purpose of prayer is to get to know God intimately, because he is an intimate God. As our intimacy with him grows, we increasingly know what he wants us to do to serve his purposes.

God is not your spiritual Santa Claus. His life's mission isn't to give you everything you think you want. He is not checking his list; he's certainly not checking it twice, because his response to your prayer requests does not depend solely on whether you're naughty or nice.

God is not the rich guy in the sky waiting to meet all your lavish requests for travel, luxury, and comfort in exchange for spending a little quality time with you.

God is not your spiritual drive-through window. Have you noticed we can treat him like that? We mostly ignore him until we need something, then we remember, "Oh yeah, prayer!" So you pull up to the little box, push the button, and place your order. "God, here's what I need . . ." You pull your car around and expect whatever you asked for to be given to you immediately.

We need to understand that God is not a benefactor in the sky or a button to be pushed but a relationship to be pursued. God is love. He created us to receive his love and to love him back. He made us for a relationship with him, and every relationship has communication at its core. God is love, and prayer is his language. We pray because we want to know God more. We want to become more like him. Again, the purpose of prayer is not to get God to do our will. The purpose of prayer is to know God so we can do *his* will.

You might object and say, "But Jesus told us to ask. We looked at that verse in John 14 where he said we should!" Yes, he did. And we should. God loves us so much he wants us to ask. And because he loves us, he loves to give us what we ask for, and he often does. But that is not the purpose of prayer.

Think of it this way: What if I thought the purpose of marriage was to ask Amy to do things for me and for her to give me whatever I want? We for sure wouldn't call it marriage, and we certainly wouldn't call it love. Now, it is true that I sometimes ask Amy to do things for me, and because she loves me, she often does what I ask. Yet that is only an aspect of our relationship, not a significant one, and definitely not its purpose.

In the same way, you can ask God for things (and he wants you to), but that is not the purpose of prayer.

Again, you may object and say, "But Jesus didn't just tell us to ask. He said, 'You may ask me for anything in my name, and I will do it.' He promised to answer our prayers! But sometimes he doesn't. So was Jesus lying?"

That question may be the cause of some of your gravest doubts:

- I prayed for my mother to be healed, and she wasn't. Why didn't God answer my prayer?
- I prayed for a new job, but I don't have one. Why didn't God give me that? What about that promise from Jesus?
- I asked God to send me a spouse and I'm still alone. Does he really care? Is he even there?

These are serious concerns with weighty questions that have caused some sincere people to walk away from their faith.

So what's the answer?

I can't tell you why God didn't do what he could have done. But I have a few thoughts that might help.

Let me start by saying that we need to be careful about building a theology around one verse. We want to understand and interpret each verse in its context and within the context of the whole Bible.

It's dangerous to pluck one verse, especially out of context, and construct your entire understanding on that. We want to get the big picture of what the Bible says to make sure we're understanding that one verse correctly.

So here's what I propose we do. Let's look at what God tells us about answering prayer in a variety of verses, to let the Bible interpret the Bible. And I think we'll find some potential reasons why God doesn't always answer our prayers the way we want. Let's walk through four possible reasons God didn't do what you asked him to do.

Reason 1: A Broken Relationship

Jesus was talking to one of his disciples about faith and prayer.

He spoke of the power of prayer, saying that if you have faith, you can ask for something as crazy as a mountain to be moved and God will make it happen.

Then Jesus says, "Therefore I tell you, whatever you ask for in prayer, believe that you have received it, and it will be yours" (Mark 11:24).

There Jesus goes again, making big promises about God answering prayer. This verse sounds a lot like the other one we read.

But then he says something interesting: "And when you stand praying, if you hold anything against anyone, forgive them, so that your Father in heaven may forgive you your sins" (Mark 11:25).

He said something similar in Matthew 5:23–24: "Therefore, if you are offering your gift at the altar and there remember that your brother or sister has something against you, leave your gift there in front of the altar. First go and be reconciled to them; then come and offer your gift."

And then later Peter, who was one of Jesus' best friends and who learned everything from him, instructed husbands to "be considerate as you live with your wives, and treat them with respect . . ."—check this out—"so that nothing will hinder your prayers" (1 Peter 3:7).

It seems our relationships with other people matter when we pray to God.

If you have children, you get that. Let's say your kids are fighting. They're screaming at each other. They come running in yelling, "She pulled my hair!" "Well, he called me a brat-rat loser-boozer!" Then they ask, "Can we have friends over tonight?" What's your answer? No. "Can we get pizza for dinner?" No.

Why?

Because they're fighting.

Do you love them less? Of course not. Do you want to bless them? Of course you do. But they're not doing what you asked, and you want them to treat each other right.

You would tell them, "Now is not the time to be asking me for anything. First, get things right between you. Love each other the way we do in our family, and then come back to me."

That's pretty much exactly what Jesus said. "*First* go and be reconciled." It's as if he were saying, *First things first, and what's first is loving me and loving people, not the wish list of things you're hoping I'll give you to make your life better. What's most important is who you are becoming, not which blessings you receive. The priority is how you're living and how you're loving other people, not what you're longing for.*

You might remember a time when you asked God to do something, but he didn't. Perhaps you also harbored bitterness toward someone or had a relationship you hadn't tried to reconcile. Maybe God wanted you to seek relational healing first, then come back and ask him again.

So why didn't our prayers get answered the way we expected?

Maybe a broken relationship needs to be mended.

Reason 2: A Wrong Motive

I have a history of praying selfish prayers. In college, I may have prayed for several cute girls who were far from God to come to faith in Jesus. *Wait, that's not selfish.* It is if your motivation is to be able to date those cute girls. I'm embarrassed to admit that's true.

I wonder whether you sometimes pray with the wrong motives. (It wouldn't be unusual if you did. I'm guessing most everyone prays with the wrong motives at least occasionally.)

The Pharisees did. All the time. They wore impressive robes and stood on the street corners praying long, elaborate prayers. Their prayers weren't for God but for status and the applause of people, so Jesus exposed them, saying, "Everything they do is done for people to see" (Matt. 23:5), and then he said to them, "Woe to you, teachers of the law and Pharisees, you hypocrites! You are like whitewashed tombs, which look beautiful on the outside but on the inside are full of the bones of the dead and everything unclean. In the same way, on the outside you appear to people as righteous but on the inside you are full of hypocrisy and wickedness" (vv. 27–28).

I doubt you pray long, flowing prayers on a street corner wearing a long, flowing robe, but I think we all occasionally ask God with the wrong motives. If we do, it affects whether God will answer.

James addressed this too. After writing, "You desire but do not have" and "You covet but you cannot get what you want" (James 4:2), he continues, "You do not have because you do not ask God. When you ask, you do not receive, because you ask with wrong motives, that you may spend what you get on your pleasures" (vv. 2–3).

"Pleasures" is translated from a word that connotes adultery. The very next words James writes are "You adulterous people" (v. 4).

Pastor J. D. Greear describes this in a way that makes a lot of sense to me:

> Imagine a man approaches his wife and says, "When we married, you pledged to fulfill my romantic needs. . . . What I have determined I need romantically is your friend Katy. Can you arrange a date with her for me?"
>
> This man is not going to receive a positive answer to his request. . . . We pray like adulterers when we ask God for something to fulfill a need in us that we should be finding in God. When I need the job, the health, the marriage partner, the restored relationship so that I can have joy, God says, *Why are you not finding your joy in me?*[2]

It doesn't make sense for God to give us what we want if it keeps us from recognizing what we really need: him.

It also doesn't make sense for God to give us what we want if it's just a selfish request. God wants to lead us away from selfishness, not enable it.

Why didn't God respond to that request the way you'd hoped?

Maybe you have a broken relationship that needs to be mended or you're asking with a wrong motive.

Reason 3: A Lack of Faith

What if you ask God to do something but don't believe he can, or will?

There was a dad in the Bible who had a son who was possessed by an evil spirit. This boy couldn't talk, would foam at the mouth, and would get tossed all over, even thrown into fires. The father was beside himself and asked Jesus' disciples, "Hey, you guys hang out with Jesus. You have power. Can you cast out this demon?" The disciples tried but couldn't do it.

Jesus showed up, and the dad explained the situation to him and asked for help. "It has often thrown him into fire or water to kill him. But if you can do anything, take pity on us and help us" (Mark 9:22). Jesus responded, "'If you can'? . . . Everything is possible for one who believes" (v. 23). And "immediately the boy's father exclaimed, 'I do believe; help me overcome my unbelief!'" (v. 24).

I love this guy's honesty. He's like, "I do believe! Well, kinda. I mean, I have belief. But I also have unbelief." I appreciate that, because sometimes I feel as if I have faith *and* don't have faith at the same time.

Can you relate?

Jesus healed the guy's kid and then "the disciples came to Jesus in private and asked, 'Why couldn't we drive it out?'" (Matt. 17:19). Jesus' response? "Because you have so little faith" (v. 20).

In one sense, that is so hard for me to understand. These disciples had seen Jesus do all kinds of amazing miracles, so how could they "have so little faith"?

At the same time, it makes sense. In fact, I relate to it. Because at times my faith is so small, so weak. Yet I have seen God do miraculous things.

As I mentioned earlier, I've seen God heal blindness. I've witnessed people have their stage-four terminal cancer vanish. I've seen God provide for people in miraculous ways and give alcoholics sobriety. I know people everyone thought to be hopeless sinners and cynics, but God radically transformed them.

In my lifetime, God has answered prayer after prayer after prayer, but there's one specific terminal illness I won't name that God has never said yes to my petition for healing. Seven or eight times over thirty years we were asked to pray for someone with this particular disease.

Every time, we prayed.

Every time, we believed God for healing.

And, every time, we went to the person's funeral.

At one point, Amy and I got a call—another person had that same terminal illness. We were asked to go to his house to pray. We arrived, and the family asked, "Pastor Craig, would you pray?" I paused, looked at the man, and responded, "I think Amy would love to pray."

I'm embarrassed to admit it but, even though I knew God could heal that man, in that moment I just didn't have the faith to pray.

That is a problem. Because our faith really matters to God. Not only is faith what makes us right with him, but also "without faith it is impossible to please God" (Heb. 11:6).

We just read a story about a man who admitted he only kind of had faith. In Matthew 9, two blind men called out to Jesus for healing, and he asked them, "'Do you believe that I am able to do this?' 'Yes, Lord,' they replied. Then he touched their eyes and said, 'According to your faith let it be done to you'; and their sight was restored" (Matt. 9:28–30).

Jesus said, "According to your *faith*."

He also healed a woman who had a serious illness for twelve years. What allowed her desperate prayer to be answered? Jesus said, "Your faith has healed you" (Mark 5:34).

Another time, Jesus went to his hometown. The people there didn't believe in him because they remembered when he was a kid. We're told, "He could not do any miracles there, except lay his hands on a few sick people and heal them" (Mark 6:5). Why just a few? "And he did not do many miracles there because of their lack of faith" (Matt. 13:58). In fact, "he was amazed at their lack of faith" (Mark 6:6).

Your faith matters to God.

At the same time, we need to remember that God is always God. When we doubt and don't believe, he is still God. I am not suggesting a prosperity gospel that claims, "If you have enough faith, God has to do what you want him to do. He has to heal you, bless you, he'll even make you rich—if only you have enough faith." I don't believe that, because it's a self-centered distortion of what the Bible teaches. It's an attempt to control God and put faith in ourselves instead of in our God. Having enough faith does not force God's hand, and he won't bless our selfishness.

> EVEN WHEN WE DOUBT AND DON'T BELIEVE, GOD IS STILL GOD.

At the same time, we understand that because our faith matters to God, we need to pray with faith.

So if you pray and God doesn't answer your prayer, you might have a broken relationship, you might need a motive check, it might be time to strengthen your faith, or God might have a better idea.

Reason 4: A Better Idea

What if there are times when God doesn't answer your prayer because he has something different in mind? What if he has a better idea?

I love the promise we're made in 1 John 5:14–15: "This is the confidence we have in approaching God: that if we ask anything according to his will, he hears us. And if we know that he hears us—whatever we ask—we know that we have what we asked of him."

You can be confident that God hears you. As I confessed before, you may also sometimes feel as if he's ignoring you, but he is not. So why didn't he do what you asked him to do? He might know something you don't know. God is sovereign and omniscient and omnipresent, right? What if he has a better answer than the one you're wanting? Maybe what you value isn't as valuable as what he values?

In the Bible we read that the apostle Paul had what he called a "thorn in [his] flesh" that "tormented" him (2 Cor. 12:7). We don't know what the thorn was. Some think it was an eye problem, as Paul mentioned several times that he didn't have good eyesight. Others guess it might have been malaria or migraines or epilepsy. Because Paul repeatedly stated that he was not eloquent, some wonder if he had a speech impediment. Others wonder if it was an evil person who made his life hell. We don't know what the thorn was, but we do know Paul prayed for God to remove it. "Three times I pleaded with the Lord to take it away from me" (v. 8).

I can picture Paul begging God, "Lord, would you take this away? I know you can. I've seen you do the miraculous for so many people. God, this is tormenting me. It's slowing me down. Please, take this away."

This is Paul, who encountered the risen Christ and faithfully preached the gospel for thirty years city by city around the Mediterranean. Paul, who served Jesus so faithfully that he was persecuted, beaten, stoned, and imprisoned. This is Paul, whom God used to heal diseases, cast out demons, and raise the dead. This is Paul, who wrote a quarter of the New Testament. *That's* who is praying this prayer.

I bet when he prayed for God to remove his thorn, Paul's relationships, as far as they depended on him, were healthy. And that his motives were pure. We know Paul had an incredibly strong faith. But, even still, God did not do what Paul asked: "But he said to me, 'My grace is sufficient for you, for my power is made perfect in weakness.' Therefore I will boast all the more gladly about my weaknesses, so that Christ's power may rest on me. That is why, for Christ's sake, I delight in weaknesses, in insults, in hardships, in persecutions, in difficulties. For when I am weak, then I am strong" (2 Cor. 12:9–10).

Paul realized that what he valued—being free of his tormenting thorn—was not as valuable as what God valued—experiencing God's sufficiency in his insufficiency and God's power in his weakness.

So did Paul get angry and quit, end his ministry and walk away, or start the first chapter of the deconstruction movement? No. Not getting what he asked for changed Paul's perspective. Instead of bemoaning his weaknesses, he boasted and delighted in them. If you asked Paul, he'd tell you God not answering his prayer was the best thing that could have happened. In fact, he would have prayed for God not to take away his thorn if he knew it was God's will.

Tim Keller says it this way in his book *Prayer*: "God will either give us what we ask or give us what we would have asked if we knew everything he knows."[3]

Can you look back and see times when God didn't give you what you wanted because he wanted to give you something better?

You wanted that certain job but got one you loved more.

You hoped to marry that person you thought you were crazy about but years later are so glad you didn't.

You prayed for your child to have that one big opportunity but later realized God had something better planned.

How about what you're asking him for now?

It might be a new house or job. Maybe a spouse. Or for God to remove an annoying person from your life. Maybe, like Paul, you have a "thorn" you've been asking God to remove. You've prayed three times. Okay, more like 333 times! But it still hasn't happened. You don't understand. It's causing you to ask some legitimate questions, which God welcomes. But is it possible he is not giving you what you want because he wants to give you something better? Or his timing is going to turn out to be far better than your timing? Maybe he wants you to realize that he is enough and his grace is all you need.

That's what Amy and I discovered with the loss of her brother, David. It's been more than two decades since he went to heaven and so we can talk about it today without the extreme grief we endured during the early years.

David had a singing voice straight from heaven. If *American Idol* had been a thing when he was alive, he'd have been a strong contender.

Because God used David to touch so many people through his worship leading, his funeral was packed with family and friends.

My pastor Nick and I shared the honor of officiating the service. Toward the end, David's wife, Paula, spoke about his faith. Then I asked whether anyone wanted to follow Jesus. And David and Amy's uncle—who had never shown any interest in God, whom we had all prayed for consistently for years—put his faith in Jesus. His life, now and for eternity, was totally changed. For years we heard story after story of how David's life *and death* changed so many lives.

One day we were reflecting on our family's loss, and I asked Amy, very gently, "With all the lives changed by David's story, would you undo all of it if you could have him back?" Without hesitation, the sister who deeply grieved her brother's death said firmly, "No way would I change it. David is in heaven. We will see him again. And we'll see so many more people there one day because of him."

I fell silent in agreement.

When God doesn't answer your prayer, though it may not make any sense at the time, he might just have something different in mind. Like a better idea.

Perhaps someday you'll realize with gratitude that God not answering your prayer was the best thing that could have possibly happened.

Why Bother?

By now you may be wondering, *Why bother?*

After all, as I said, prayer can feel complicated and confusing. And now I've told you that you need to have the right motives and enough faith. And it just seems like God is going to do whatever he wants anyway.

So why bother praying?

Because prayer isn't about getting things from God. It's more beautiful than that. Prayer is about intimacy with a God who knows you, loves you more than you can imagine, and is inviting you to partner with him in his mission and give you an adventure.

Prayer isn't about trying to control God; it's about giving him control. We don't pray to force God's hand; we pray to seek his face. Remember that the purpose of prayer is not to get God to do our will. The purpose of prayer is to know God so we can do his will.

> **"This, then, is how you should pray: 'Our Father in heaven, hallowed be your name, your kingdom come, your will be done, on earth as it is in heaven.'"**
> —MATTHEW 6:9-10

CHAPTER 4 EXERCISE

1. On a scale of 1 (you never pray) to 10 (you pray regularly and believe God hears and answers), how would you rate your faith in prayer? Explain your answer.
2. Like my wife and I had with her brother's death, have you had a challenging, confusing experience with God not answering a prayer the way you wanted him to? Explain.
3. What are your thoughts on this statement: "The purpose of prayer is not to get God to do our will. The purpose of prayer is to know God so we can do his will"?

In questions 4 through 10, we'll apply the reasons I gave that the Bible offers for why prayers go unanswered.

4. Considering "Reason 1: A Broken Relationship," are there any relationships you need to get right to realign your prayer life?
5. Considering "Reason 2: A Wrong Motive," are there any selfish prayers you know you need to address and correct?
6. Considering "Reason 3: A Lack of Faith," is there a circumstance in which you have little belief left or have even given up hoping for an answer to prayer?
7. In the story of Jesus in Mark 9, how might the boy's father's answer of "I do believe; help me overcome my unbelief!" help or encourage you in your prayer life?
8. Considering "Reason 4: A Better Idea," have you ever had (or do you have) a "thorn in the flesh" in your own life? Explain.
9. Is there a prayer you once prayed that you can now look back on with gratitude that God didn't answer in the way you hoped at the time? Explain.
10. Was there a major takeaway or action point for you about prayer from this chapter? Explain.

CHAPTER 5

Why Would God Provide Only One Way?

"In" versus "Ex"

What's not to like about Jesus?

Right?

He loved everyone.

He showed compassion to hurting people.

He humbled oppressive leaders.

He shared powerful insights on how to live a better life.

He served the needy.

He gave grace to people caught in sin.

He defended poor widows.

He provided barrels of wine to thirsty wedding guests and filet-o-fish sandwiches to a huge crowd of people who hadn't eaten and were getting hangry.

So what's not to like about Jesus?

Well, there is the whole exclusive thing.

We like *inclusive*.

In is better than *ex*.

Ex means out and *in* means, well, in. And we'd all rather be in than out.

Think about it. Would you rather be *in*vited or *ex*iled? Included or expelled? And don't even get me started on the possibility of being executed, exterminated, or excommunicated. Also, anyone want to become extinct? I don't think so.

In is clearly better than *ex*. So what's not to like about Jesus?

The exclusive claims are easy to get hung up on, like these:

- Jesus is the only way to God.
- Jesus is the one way to be forgiven.
- Jesus is the exclusive way to heaven.

Wait. Who said Jesus is the only way?

He did.

The Bold Claim

Throughout the ages, people have made bold "I am" claims.

Muhammad Ali declared, "I am the greatest."

Michael Jordan stated, "I am the best."

Popeye claimed, "I am what I am." (Technically, it was "I yam what I yam.")

Then there was that tree thing in *Guardians of the Galaxy* that would not stop proclaiming, "I am Groot."

And, more recently, Billie Eilish sang, "I think, therefore I am" (echoing French philosopher René Descartes, who said it about four hundred years ago).

Are you ready for the boldest "I am" statement ever?

Jesus said, "I am the way and the truth and the life. No one comes to the Father except through me" (John 14:6).

The way? Not a way. *A* way is fine. But *the* way? Like no one else could ever be another way or find another way? *That* is exclusive.

And "the truth" and "the life"? What does that even mean? Is Jesus suggesting he is the one standard of truth? The only source of life?

Jesus compounded the issue with the next sentence. "No one" can come to the Father "except through" him? We've all heard it said that there are many paths to God. That people of different faiths can coexist knowing that we're all actually worshiping the same god and will all end up in the same place.

We often hear it said, "You're good as long as you believe in something." That is *in*finitely *in*clusive and sounds *in*credibly *in*viting. But Jesus shutting out everyone from God unless they come through him? That seems *ex*ceedingly *ex*clusive and *ex*tremely *ex*acting.

Have you ever said something you didn't really mean because you were in a weird mood? I have! Lest we think Jesus was maybe just having one of those days when he said the whole "I am the way, truth, life, no one comes to the Father without me" thing, we need to be aware of Jesus' other bold statements. For instance, within ten chapters of the book of John, he said:

- "I am the bread of life. Whoever comes to me will never go hungry, and whoever believes in me will never be thirsty" (6:35).
- "I am the light of the world. Whoever follows me will never walk in darkness, but will have the light of life" (8:12).
- "I am the good shepherd. The good shepherd lays down his life for the sheep" (10:11).
- "I am the resurrection and the life. The one who believes in me will live, even though they die; and whoever lives by believing in me will never die. Do you believe this?" (11:25–26).
- "I am the vine; you are the branches. If you remain in me and I in you, you will bear much fruit; apart from me you can do nothing" (15:5).

As if all of these "I am" statements weren't enough, there's the time Jesus said, "I and the Father are one" (John 10:30). And check out these audacious words Jesus spoke: "Anyone who loves their father or mother more than me is not worthy of me; anyone who loves their son or daughter more than me is not worthy of me. Whoever does not take up their cross and follow me is not worthy of me" (Matt. 10:37–38).

Wow, Jesus, my mom?! Seriously? And my kids too? I mean, I don't want to seem blasphemous, but don't you realize people prefer a little more lenience? Why draw such a hard line?

What I've found is that the exclusive claims of Jesus are one of the primary objections people have about him. They like the way he lived. They like the way he loved. They're just not crazy about what he claimed.

When I say "people," I realize that might include you. And if so, I get it. You struggle to understand how a loving God would provide only one way to him and heaven. When you hear someone say that all paths lead to God, it sounds compassionate, and you want to be compassionate. After all, aren't followers of Jesus supposed to be compassionate? So shouldn't we take the position that gives hope to more people? Isn't it incomprehensible that we wouldn't be more inclusive?

And here's another "in" word: intelligent. It seems reasonable to think that various faith-filled people around the world are at least right in some aspect of their beliefs. But it feels incredible to claim that one relatively small group of believers has the corner on truth and everyone else is wrong. And if that is our claim, and we count ourselves among the few who have it right, isn't that arrogant? Should Jesus' followers be arrogant?

Maybe that's why people aren't discouraged by the way Jesus lived or loved but have doubts about what he claimed.

Everyone likes Jesus, but let's not go overboard.

Yet as followers of Jesus, aren't we supposed to go overboard? Just read the book of Acts.

We do believe Jesus is the way, the truth, and the life. We're convinced he is the only way to God and that people who believe in him will live even though they die.

But there are a lot of buts. Like, "Yeah, I believe that . . ."

- But only as long as you're sincere.
- But don't all paths lead to the same God?
- But isn't that arrogant?
- But isn't God unfair?

Here's something I didn't expect to write when I started this book: Let's take a look at the buts. Let's talk about those buts.

Looking at all the questions we just raised, let's see whether we can find some answers that overcome our doubts and maybe even give us a more *int*ellectually sound and *int*egrated faith.

But Only as Long as You're Sincere

People like to say "What really matters is not what you believe but the sincerity of your faith. You can believe whatever you want to believe, but only as long as you're sincere."

People will make this claim about the most important belief in their lives—what they put their faith in for their salvation and eternal destiny—but they wouldn't apply it to anything else that's important to them. Here's what I mean.

Your friend shares with you, "I've been saving money for years. I've got a good amount in the bank and a lot in retirement. I had a cashier at the Dollar Store tell me about a stock. I asked my uncle, who is a stockbroker, and he told me it's a horrible investment. But, well, I just believe that if I put all my money into it, I'll be rich!" You look your friend in the eye and say, "You're going to put *everything* in it? I think you should do it. As long as your faith in the stock is sincere, it will be a great investment." No!

Your friend confides in you, "I need to have surgery, and my Uber driver from the other day said he could do it for me. He's not a doctor and has never done surgery, but I believe he can do it!" You smile at your friend and say, "Well, as long as you sincerely believe he can!" Um, no.

Can you recall the last time you were sincere but wrong? Sincerely mistaken?

What matters is not the sincerity of your faith but the trustworthiness of what you put your faith in.

Here's another illustration: You and a friend are standing at the edge of a frozen pond. You're confident the ice is frozen solid enough to hold you if you were to walk out on it. Your friend isn't so sure. Someone else shows up, hears the dilemma, and says, "What matters is the sincerity of your faith. If you really believe the ice is strong enough, it will hold you." Then the person turns to your friend and says, "And if you don't sincerely believe it, it won't."

> **WHAT MATTERS IS NOT THE SINCERITY OF YOUR FAITH BUT THE TRUSTWORTHINESS OF WHAT YOU PUT YOUR FAITH IN.**

That person is wrong. Ridiculously wrong.

If the ice is thick enough, it will hold you up with your fully assured faith *and* it will hold up your friend with his uncertain faith. If the ice isn't thick enough, your doubting friend will fall through it and so will you, even with your sincere faith!

The issue is not whether your faith is sincere but whether the object of your faith is worthy of your faith.

We all put our faith in something. I would encourage you to put yours in something strong enough to hold you up.

But Don't All Paths Lead to the Same God?

You've heard that a lot, right? All paths lead to the same God. They're all equally valid and they're all teaching basically the same thing.

It's definitely a nice sentiment to just want everyone to get along. That's a good thing, right?

I have found that most of the world religions have some good in them. But they are not teaching the same things. So the claim that they all lead to the same God is not true. How can it be? Let me explain.

All religions are equally protected and should be. Everyone has the right to believe whatever he or she wants to believe. No one should be able to prevent anyone from believing what they want or force anyone into something they don't want to believe.

While all religions are equally protected, that does not mean they are equally valid. Anyone who claims that to be true hasn't done enough serious studying on world religions. There may be some similarities among various religions, but at their core they are dramatically different. If we're all worshiping the same God, if we're all just taking different paths to the same God, then that God is either a liar or schizophrenic.

Let me show you a few examples.

Christianity teaches that there is only one God, and he is a personal God.

Buddhism teaches that there is no God.

Hinduism teaches that there are thousands (or even millions) of gods.

Islam says God told Muhammad that every believer must make a pilgrimage to Mecca to worship.

Christianity says Jesus told us it doesn't matter where we worship.

Christianity teaches that it's okay to eat meat.

Hinduism teaches that eating meat is immoral.

Buddhism claims that after you die you get reincarnated and live another life here on earth.

Christianity claims that you live only one life, but that God has invited you to continue living with him forever in heaven.

New Age belief systems say there is no personal God and that everything in existence is connected as part of a universal whole. Our goal should be to attain to a higher consciousness to effect our own transformation.

Christianity says there is a personal God who loves us and sent his Son to sacrifice himself for us. Our goal should be to know, love, worship, and glorify God, who brings about his transformation in us.

Does that sound as though all religions are basically saying the same thing?

If your answer is no, that also means there's no way they can all be right. And how could the same God teach all of these contradicting ideas?

So are all religions basically the same? No.

Equally protected? Yes.

Equally valid? No.

Are there major differences between them? Yes.

Do they all lead to the same God? No.

Why?

Because the same God could not be telling us such contradictory things.

Can anyone believe in any religion they choose? Of course.

But even if we don't like it, the truth is that there are a lot of people whose faith is in the wrong place.

But Isn't That Arrogant?

That last sentence, "The truth is that there are a lot of people whose faith is in the wrong place," could sound smug. That's an issue people have with Christians' claim that their way is the only way. Does that make you uncomfortable? Isn't it arrogant and unloving to think you're right and everyone else is wrong?

No.

It's not arrogant or intolerant to say that you believe something is true, even that it's exclusively true.

Saying "2 + 2 = 4 and it does not equal anything else" is not arrogant or intolerant. It's just true. It just is.

And if I say, "I believe Jesus is the only way to God," that's not arrogant or intolerant. Because I believe it's true.

Now, anyone can believe or say that something is true and be arrogant about it. That is wrong. It's wrong to be arrogant. The unfortunate reality is that there are people in all religions who are arrogant about what they believe. Some even believe that if you don't believe like they believe, you deserve to die. Now, that's arrogant!

Arrogance doesn't make what you believe right or wrong, but it *is* wrong to be arrogant. The Bible says God hates pride and opposes the proud (Prov. 8:13; 1 Peter 5:5). So if a Christian is arrogant about what he believes, that *is* a problem to God.

But it is not arrogant or intolerant to say that Jesus is the only way to heaven.

Think of it this way: It would not be arrogant or intolerant to tell everyone that you've found the cure for cancer. In fact, it would be loving to let everyone know you found the cure. And if you found the only cure for cancer but didn't tell people because you didn't want to sound exclusive, that would not be loving. Actually, that would be hateful.

In the same way, love should be the only motivation for Christians sharing their belief with others that Jesus is the only way to God and heaven.

The issue isn't whether a Christian is arrogant in saying Jesus is the only way but rather whether that Christian is right. Is what they believe true?

Christianity's claim that Jesus is the only way is based not on arrogance but on objective evidence.

What's interesting is that basically every religion claims to be the only way. Christianity hasn't cornered the market on thinking it's cornered the market. Every religion claims it's the exclusively true one.

> CHRISTIANITY'S CLAIM THAT JESUS IS THE ONLY WAY IS BASED NOT ON ARROGANCE BUT ON OBJECTIVE EVIDENCE.

So if they all say they're the one right way, what do you do? Do you go with the one your parents taught you? Or with what most people in your culture believe?

No.

Because it's *your* faith. You recognize this is life's greatest and most important question, and you take it seriously. It's eternally serious. Ask the hard questions. Dig in. See whether Jesus is who he claims to be. Decide for yourself what you believe about the one who made all the "I

am" statements. Determine whether his truth changes lives. If you wonder whether you can objectively discover eternal truth, the answer is yes,
you can.

This is another significant difference between Christianity and the
other world religions. Study them and you'll realize that they are based
on a philosophy taught by a person. So there's no real way of investigating
whether it's right or wrong. Should you believe what Muhammad said? Or
what Buddha said? If you want to, you can. But it's not possible to prove
that their teachings are true, because their teachings are just their ideas
about God.

That's where Christianity is different in at least four key aspects,
based on the following:

- The experience of grace
- The evidence of historical events
- The teachings of Jesus
- The resurrection of Jesus

Christianity begs to be investigated. You can go back and find out
whether the events described in the Bible really happened. Jesus told
people he would die and then on the third day rise from the dead (Matt.
16:21–23; 17:22–23; 20:17–19). Then Jesus died and three days later
walked out of the grave alive. *That* is what a Christian's faith is based on.

Christianity is not just centered on the teachings of Jesus, it's based
on the resurrection of Jesus.

Paul writes that this is the "gospel" by which "you are saved" (1 Cor.
15:2). What is that gospel? "That Christ died for our sins according to the
Scriptures, that he was buried, that he was raised on the third day according to the Scriptures" (1 Cor. 15:3–4).

The truth of the gospel is based on the resurrection, as Paul taught:
"And if Christ has not been raised, our preaching is useless and so is your
faith. More than that, we are then found to be false witnesses about God,
for we have testified about God that he raised Christ from the dead. . . .

And if Christ has not been raised, your faith is futile; you are still in your sins. Then those also who have fallen asleep in Christ are lost. If only for this life we have hope in Christ, we are of all people most to be pitied" (1 Cor. 15:14–15, 17–19).

Paul was explaining that we believe, not because we have faith in the teachings and philosophy of Jesus but because Jesus proved he was who he claimed to be by defeating death. If Jesus didn't rise from the dead, then everything we believe is moot. But if he did rise from the dead, then he has proven himself trustworthy and we should put our faith in him.

To quote Tim Keller again, "If Jesus rose from the dead, then you have to accept all that he said; if he didn't rise from the dead, then why worry about any of what he said? The issue on which everything hangs is not whether or not you like his teaching but whether or not he rose from the dead."[1]

The cool thing is that you *can* prove Jesus rose from the dead. All kinds of incredibly intelligent people have tried to disprove the resurrection only to conclude that Jesus really did walk out of the grave alive, just as he'd promised, and because of that evidence he really is the only way to God.[2]

God provided one way in Jesus. Christians believe that not out of arrogance but from evidence.

But Isn't God Unfair?

If you are wrestling with your faith about everyone having to find just one way, you might also be struggling with a broader question, "If this is true, isn't God unfair?"

But I believe this is the wrong question.

Track with me on this.

Assume that this is all true:

- God is love, so he created people to love him and be in relationship with him.
- Every single person said no to God and rebelled against him by choosing selfishness and sin instead of love and holiness.

- In response, God sent his Son from heaven not to condemn people as they deserve but to save them.
- People rejected the Son of God, mocked, tortured, and murdered him.
- Then God, instead of killing off the people as they deserve, accepted the sacrifice of his Son as the punishment for the sins of the people who were responsible for his death.

If this is what God has done (and this *is* what God has done), could you look him in the eye and say, "That's not fair. You haven't done enough"?

I don't think so.

I think the right question is not "Why is there only one way?" but "Why did God provide any way?"

That's the question I have trouble answering.

> THE RIGHT QUESTION IS NOT "WHY IS THERE ONLY ONE WAY?" BUT "WHY DID GOD PROVIDE ANY WAY?"

Instead of focusing on Jesus claiming to be the only way, perhaps we should shift our perspective and be grateful that he provided a way at all.

I know the answer is wrapped up in his unfathomable love. "But God demonstrates his own love for us in this: While we were still sinners, Christ died for us" (Rom. 5:8).

Jesus died for us because it was the only way. The only way for us to be saved was through Jesus going to the cross to take our sin and experience death in our place. And God loves you so much that he was willing to have his Son do that. Jesus is so passionate about you he would rather die than live without you. So he did.

And that highlights the biggest difference between Christianity and the other religions, what could be called the "do versus done" distinction. People who have carefully studied the world's religions point out that all but one could essentially be spelled D-O.

Other world religions are based on people doing something to somehow earn the good favor of God. It might be that you have to go on a pilgrimage, or give to the poor, or carefully maintain a certain diet, or perform good deeds, or chant the right words, or use a Tibetan prayer wheel, or go through a series of reincarnations to continually improve your karma. You strive to reach up to God and earn his favor. It's about what you do for him.

By contrast, Christianity is the one religion spelled D-O-N-E. It is based not on what we do but on what Jesus has already done for us on the cross. The Bible teaches that we have all rebelled against God, but God loves us anyway. So Jesus came down from heaven and died on the cross as our substitute to offer us forgiveness of our sins, a relationship with God, and eternal life in heaven. Christianity is all about God reaching down to us and offering us his unearned favor. It's all about what he's done for us (Rom. 5:8–11).

Of the four aspects of Christianity I shared previously, the first on the list was grace, which is unique to Christianity. And that grace changed my life.

If someone still insists God is not fair, maybe there's one sense in which I'd have to agree. What do I mean?

I've done so many things wrong. I've lied, lusted, cheated, gossiped, hated, cussed, envied, boasted, judged, been selfish and arrogant, gotten drunk, and hurt people. Based on my actions, what do I deserve? I deserve spiritual death.

So if you say God's not fair, you may be right. Because if he were fair, I would have gotten what my sins deserved. But Jesus paid the price so I could be forgiven, redeemed, and set free.

That's called grace.

Why did he do this for me? Why would he do it for you?

Because he is love. It's that simple.

Love isn't just what he feels for you.

Love is not just what he does.

Love is who he is.

Down deep, isn't that what you really want? To experience unconditional, perfect love?

Isn't it possible the reason you've craved love your entire life is because God made you for love?

He made you in love, for his love.

And if he gave us a way—even just one way—to experience that love, to have that love, I say we should take it.

> I have been crucified with Christ and I no longer live, but Christ lives in me. The life I now live in the body, I live by faith in the Son of God, who loved me and gave himself for me.
>
> —Galatians 2:20

CHAPTER 5 EXERCISE

1. What are your thoughts about our culture's insistence on inclusion and issues with exclusion in Christianity?
2. Did you (or do you) struggle with Jesus' "I am" claims? Explain.
3. What are your thoughts on the "But Only as Long as You're Sincere" section? Have you ever experienced this mindset?
4. Consider the section "But Don't All Paths Lead to the Same God?" Why do you suppose this belief seems to have become more prevalent today?
5. How much were you aware of the differences between Christianity and the other major religions of the world? How did this section affect your understanding of Jesus' claim to be the only way?
6. Have you ever struggled with or experienced religious arrogance?
7. Why does the resurrection make a crucial difference between Christianity and the other world religions?
8. In the section "But Isn't God Unfair?" were any of the teaching points helpful to give you a better grasp of the gospel? Explain.
9. What are the differences between a D-O religion versus a D-O-N-E religion? Which version do you prefer, and why?
10. Consider the statement "The right question is not 'Why is there only one way?' but 'Why did God provide any way?'" How might this thought affect your faith and also motivate you to share your faith?

CHAPTER 6

Why Believe in Jesus When His Followers Are Such Hypocrites?

I don't blame Chloe or Grant. They were both strong Christians. They read their Bibles faithfully, worshiped at church passionately, and served with joy helping others to know the love of Jesus. Today, tragically, they don't know what they believe. Chloe told me she wants to believe in God but doesn't know whether she can after what happened. Grant, on the other hand, believes in some form of spirituality, but certainly not Christianity.

Why are these two previously committed followers of Jesus now so far from God? Like so many others, they were hurt and disillusioned by Christians.

For Chloe, it was her youth pastor. He was hired by her church when she'd just started her seventh-grade year at school. Like most preteens, Chloe fought to fit in. She wore the right shoes, listened to the right music, followed the right people on TikTok, and had Snapchat streaks with three of the coolest girls in her class. But even with so much that seemed right, Chloe battled ongoing anxiety and severe depression. When she opened up to her youth pastor about her problem with self-harm, he listened without any judgment whatsoever. She felt heard, understood, accepted, and loved.

While God intended for Chloe's youth pastor to change her life, the forces of darkness ultimately used him to hurt her more than she ever imagined possible. He crossed a line no one ever should. What started as sincere and appropriate acceptance grew to dangerous and inappropriate touching. First it was long hugs. Then back rubs. Then leg rubs. Then— you get the picture.

Chloe told me she "knows" she can no longer trust men and is fairly sure she can't trust God either. Because, after all, wasn't he the one who allowed her youth pastor to take advantage of her?

The problem for Grant was his father, who was also his hero. Grant's dad was successful in business, committed as a father, and strong in his faith with Jesus. Every Sunday, he took the family to church. That spiritual consistency gave Grant a deep sense of security. No matter what was going on in his life, his dad knew what to say to make things better.

But something slowly started to change as Grant became a teenager. He began noticing some of his father's inconsistencies. What once seemed spiritually helpful started to become narrow and occasionally harsh. It got worse when his dad discovered Grant had looked at porn on his phone three times. His father exploded on him in what felt like irrational rage. Already feeling the shame of his failure, Grant took the punishment as best he could. But then, two weeks later, his dad's dark secret got exposed. To everyone's shock, Grant's father had been cheating on his wife for years by sleeping with men. Many different men.

"I hate him," Grant told me, fighting back tears. "I hate him with all my heart. My 'godly' dad," he said, his words dripping with sarcasm, "said he was committed to Jesus and my mom, but he was only out for himself. His whole life was a lie."

Both Chloe and Grant had loved God with their whole hearts.

Now they resented him.

They ultimately blame God for what happened at the hands of trusted leaders who were supposed to protect them.

False Advertising?

Having been around since the 1930s, Snap, Crackle, and Pop, the three lovable characters on the Rice Krispies box, seemed like trustworthy guys. Rice Krispies was one of my favorite cereals as a kid, along with Cocoa Krispies, Frosted Flakes, Apple Jacks, and Honey Nut Cheerios. I happily ate the cereal, never stopping to ask, *What exactly are those three little smiley guys?* I guess they were equal parts onomatopoeia and elves? Chefs? Brothers? A boy band? Cousins of the seven dwarves? Okay, I admit, we don't know much about them, but they certainly seemed worthy of our trust.

Right?

Apparently not.

In 2010, Rice Krispies was accused of misleading consumers. Snap, Crackle, and Pop had been boasting on their boxes about the immunity-boosting properties of their noisy cereal, claiming it improved a child's immunity with "25 Percent Daily Value of Antioxidants and Nutrients—Vitamins A, B, C and E." Which sounds awesome. Except that it wasn't. It wasn't true.[1]

As you might expect, lawsuits followed.

Snap, Crackle, and Pop's bosses hired some big-time lawyers and settled the case out of court in 2011, paying $2.5 million to people who had believed the lie.

Let's say you were friends with Sirs Snap, Crackle, and Pop. How let down would you feel?

My guess is your life wasn't ruined by the false advertising of Kellogg's. Sure, they lied, but it's just breakfast cereal, right?

But what about bad advertising when it comes to God?

It might seem strange to think of Jesus as having a marketing department, but isn't that what his followers are? Walking, talking ads? After all, advertising is how you let people know what you're offering to persuade them to be interested. Isn't that kind of what Christians are supposed to be for Jesus?

Every Christian is called to be a bright shining light showing the world Jesus' love (Matt. 5:14–16).

Jesus said, "Love one another. As I have loved you, so you must love one another. By this everyone will know that you are my disciples, if you love one another" (John 13:34–35).

In Titus 2, Paul implores Christians to be "worthy of respect, self-controlled, and sound in faith, in love and in endurance" (v. 2) and "not to be slanderers or addicted to much wine" (v. 3) and "to be self-controlled and pure" and "kind" (v. 5). Why? "So that no one will malign the word of God" (v. 5) and that they will "have nothing bad to say about us" (v. 8). The goal? "So that in every way they will make the teaching about God our Savior attractive" (v. 10).

Sounds a lot like advertising to me.

And that is exactly the problem.

So many people have spiritual doubts, not because of Jesus, but because of his followers. Instead of showing God as he really is—full of unconditional love, unending grace, and life-giving, liberating truth—some Christians make God seem narrow-minded, harsh, judgmental, and untrustworthy.

Instead of being known for love, as Jesus commanded, his followers can be more known for what they hate and what they are against, and for being exclusive, hypercritical, and antagonistic.

1. Jesus commanded us to love our enemies (Matt. 5:44), but today people claiming to be his followers relentlessly attack their enemies on social media.
2. Jesus taught that we are to be peacemakers (Matt. 5:9), but Christians today scream hate-filled words at their protests and rallies.
3. Jesus said only those without sin can cast a stone, leading the people who wanted to punish a guilty woman to drop their weapons (John 8:1–11), but today Christians quickly and easily pick up "stones" and throw them at the guilty, and sometimes the innocent.

This reminds me of a story Jesus told in Matthew 13 known as the parable of the weeds. He said that a man sowed good seed in his field, but then that night his enemy came and sowed weeds among his wheat. As the crop began to come up, everyone saw the problem, but the man knew immediately what had happened. Wondering what to do, his servants asked him: "'Do you want us to go and pull them up?' 'No,' he answered, 'because while you are pulling the weeds, you may uproot the wheat with them. Let both grow together until the harvest. At that time I will tell the harvesters: First collect the weeds and tie them in bundles to be burned; then gather the wheat and bring it into my barn'" (Matt. 13:28–30).

Today, we still have wheat and weeds growing in the same field. But as God's servants, we don't determine the outcome. We're just supposed to take care of the crop. Only God, the one who owns the field, gets the final say. Meanwhile, God loves us all with an everlasting love. He draws people to himself with his unfailing kindness.

Tragically, though, far too many people can name off a list of hypocritical Christians who make God look unappealing, if not repulsive, instead of representing our Savior accurately and making him attractive, as Paul urged.

Here are a few common examples:

- There's the college girl who posts Bible verses nonstop on Instagram during the week, then parties hard all weekend.
- There's the boss who talks about "keeping Jesus first" but treats his employees with disrespect.
- There's the father who shames his daughter for dressing immodestly but looks at porn when his family sleeps at night.
- There's the politician who touts "godly values" but has no compassion for the "least of these"—the very people Jesus told us to serve and protect.
- The spiritual leader everyone admired until it came out that he wasn't living the life he claimed we should all be living.

Brennan Manning astutely observed, "The single greatest cause of atheism in the world today is Christians who acknowledge Jesus with their lips, then walk out the door, and deny him with their lifestyle. That is what an unbelieving world simply finds unbelievable."[2]

Hypocrites Playing a Part

Maybe you've been confused, hurt, disappointed, or disillusioned by followers of Jesus who don't seem to be anything like him.

If so, you're not alone.

Turns out Jesus didn't like it when people claimed one thing and lived another.

He *really* didn't like it.

When you look at the Gospels, you'll notice that Jesus never spoke more harshly about anyone than he did those he called "hypocrites." For instance, in Matthew 23 we find seven times when Jesus said "Woe to you" to the Pharisees, the religious leaders claiming to live in holiness but who were actually very self-absorbed and self-glorifying men. Here's one of those seven times: "Woe to you, teachers of the law and Pharisees, you hypocrites! You are like whitewashed tombs, which look beautiful on the outside but on the inside are full of the bones of the dead and everything unclean. In the same way, on the outside you appear to people as righteous but on the inside you are full of hypocrisy and wickedness" (Matt. 23:27–28).

Jesus called them hypocrites. You'll find the word *hypocrite* seventeen times in the Gospels. Every time, it was Jesus who spoke the word. And every time, he used it to describe people who "do not practice what they preach . . . everything they do is done for people to see" (Matt. 23:3).

Want to hear something interesting? Before Jesus used it, the word *hypocrite* had been used exclusively for actors, who, back then, would wear masks onstage because the same actor would play several different parts. For each character, a different mask was worn. So *hypocrite* means "one who wears a mask."

Jesus was the first person to ever use the word outside the theater context. By applying it to the Pharisees, he accused them of wearing masks, pretending to be something they weren't.

And what did Jesus say to them?

Woe. Woe. Woe. Woe. Woe. Woe. Woe.

Whoa! Jesus had a zero-tolerance policy for hypocrites.

Jesus was calling them out on their show. He already knew that, just like every other human, they were sinners. The problem he was addressing was their constant attempts to cover it up. They presented a false exterior, manipulating the impressions of others. To Jesus, their deception was what made the Pharisees hypocrites.

Jesus didn't say this:

- "Woe to you who curse when you stub your sandal on a stone."
- "Woe to you who gossip about the Romans."
- "Woe to you who drive your chariot over the speed limit."

Jesus has unlimited grace for a sinner in need of forgiveness but no tolerance for hypocrisy.

> JESUS HAS UNLIMITED GRACE FOR A SINNER IN NEED OF FORGIVENESS BUT NO TOLERANCE FOR HYPOCRISY.

Jesus said, *Woe to you hypocrites, who do the wrong things but act like you don't.* Then, just in case anyone had any doubt what he thought, Jesus told them, "You snakes! You brood of vipers! How will you escape being condemned to hell?" (Matt. 23:33).

Say it again: *whoa!*

C'mon, Jesus, tell us how you really feel.

If you've been frustrated, turned off, or disgusted by Christians who say one thing and do another, Jesus is with you.

The fact is he condemned hypocrites. But many people today who claim to follow him could be described as hypocrites. So this raises a question: Why do so many Christians get it wrong?

Let me offer three reasons.

Maybe They're Not Really Christians

First, some who claim Christ are not really Christians. These folks may be church members who carry a Bible and have a fish symbol on the bumper of their car but have never truly put their faith in or been forgiven or transformed by Jesus. They're described this way in Titus 1:16: "They claim to know God, but by their actions they deny him."

Just to clarify:

- Going to church doesn't make you a Christian. Following Jesus does.
- Attending a Bible study doesn't make you a Christian. Following Jesus does.
- Believing in God doesn't make you a Christian. Following Jesus does.
- Getting baptized doesn't make you a Christian. Following Jesus does.

Why do so many of those who claim to be Christians do things that are horrible, such as betray and hurt others and malign the name of Jesus? Maybe because many of them are not actually Christians.

When I was in high school, my family moved to a small town in southern Oklahoma. Everyone there looked up to a respected schoolteacher who also taught Sunday school at church.

Tragically, in secret, he started grooming my little sister in the sixth grade and sexually abused her and other young girls repeatedly.

I cannot know whether he ever had genuine faith, but I do know this, applying Titus 1:16: he claimed to know God but by his actions he denied him.

Sadly, there are many who claim Christ but do not know him. Yes, there are those in positions of spiritual leadership who don't know him. Jesus told us he will respond to many who call him "Lord" on the day of judgment by saying, "I never knew you. Away from me, you evildoers!" (Matt. 7:23).

In Jesus' parable of the sheep and the goats in Matthew 25:31–46, we see that both responded to the King with a question that began with the same words: "Lord, when did we see you . . . ?" *Both* addressed Jesus as Lord. The difference? The sheep showed consistent evidence of Jesus' work in their lives, while the goats did not.

The people who call him Lord but do evil are a big part of the reason too many Christians are viewed as hypocrites, which then creates false advertising, distracting and diverting attention from what Jesus does in our lives.

Maybe They're Just Baby Christians

As I've mentioned, in college I was really far from God, and it showed in the way I lived my life. But I started reading the Bible and was drawn to Jesus. One day, I knelt and prayed, "God, if you're there, show me. I will give you my life." Following that simple prayer, I sincerely felt God's presence and somehow knew everything was different.

Soon I met with a good friend who was living at least as wild a life as mine and told him, "I think I've decided I'm 'religious.'" I would never say it that way today, but I was new to all of this and didn't know how to explain what was happening.

Unbeknownst to me, my friend had also just put his faith in Jesus and was trying to figure out how to tell me. I had no idea!

His response to my news? "No f***ing way!" (He was so excited for me, and he didn't know any better.) Then he shouted, "Me too!" I was like, "No f***ing way!" (I was so excited for him, and I didn't know any better either.) "That's amazing!"

We were both so pumped at our mutual decision that we just had to celebrate the only way we knew how.

We went out and got wasted.

Seriously.

That's what we did.

If you have recently decided to put your faith in Jesus, I recommend baptism as a next step, not Margarita Monday (or Tequila Tuesday, or Whiskey Wednesday). But we were brand-new followers of Jesus and didn't know any better yet.

Jesus was accused of hanging out with "sinners" who also didn't know any better yet. He met people right where they were at the time. And he still does.

I'm sharing this story because some people who misrepresent Jesus *are* Christians (such as me and my friend), but they're still brand-new or very young in their spiritual development. They are described in Hebrews 5 as baby Christians: "Anyone who lives on milk, being still an infant, is not acquainted with the teaching about righteousness. But solid food is for the mature, who by constant use have trained themselves to distinguish good from evil" (Heb. 5:13–14).

> SOME PEOPLE WHO MISREPRESENT JESUS ARE CHRISTIANS, BUT THEY'RE STILL BRAND-NEW OR VERY YOUNG IN THEIR SPIRITUAL DEVELOPMENT.

So why do some Christians do wrong things that confuse those who look at their lives and see them not representing Jesus? They *are* born of the kingdom of God, but they're still immature and growing in their faith. They have not yet learned wrong from right and how to do what's right.

While salvation is a one-time event, transformation is a lifelong journey. The Holy Spirit may come to us in a download, but, through him, change happens day by day. That means every Christian is at a unique place in his or her walk of faith.

We're Imperfect, In-Process Christians

Why do so many Christians get it wrong?

Some aren't Christians.

Some are baby Christians.

Others are Christians who are imperfect and in process.

To be clear, that's the rest of us. You and me. It's no longer "them," it's "us." We are all imperfect, in-process Christians.

Every day, even with Jesus in our lives, we can make bad choices and say bad things. We're still tempted by a very sly spiritual enemy who is always on the attack against even mature followers of Jesus. Even as we become more and more like Jesus, we still fall into sin sometimes.

When we do mess up, that doesn't mean we're hell-bound hypocrites. We genuinely love Jesus but in a weak moment tell a lie or speak harsh words. We may give in to temptation and betray someone. There is no excuse, and it is heartbreaking, but that does not necessarily mean we don't have real faith.

God has "made his light shine in our hearts . . . but we have this treasure in jars of clay" (2 Cor. 4:6–7). He knows we are weak, "for he knows how we are formed, he remembers that we are dust" (Ps. 103:14).

We are merely dust.

No matter how mature you are, you're still vulnerable. And if you think you're not, you are even more vulnerable. Pride often comes before a fall (Prov. 16:18).

All of this means we're going to let each other down. While that is a problem, I think there's an even deeper problem.

I Sin. You Sin. We All Fall Down.

Let's say someone cuts you off in traffic. Why? *The guy is a jerk who doesn't care about anyone but himself!*

Let's say you cut someone off in traffic. Why? *You didn't see the other car! You obviously wouldn't do that on purpose.*

That is a cognitive bias we all have called the fundamental attribution error, which means this:

- When we fall short, we blame our circumstances.
- When other people fall short, we blame their character.[3]
- When I sin, I might say, "I didn't mean to, I was just tired and under

a lot of pressure. And, really, it wasn't that big of a deal. Besides, you know my heart. I'm not that kind of person."

- When someone else commits the same sin, we say, "That person's so bad. I doubt he's even a Christian. What a hypocrite!"

In a sermon I was preaching, I wanted to illustrate the selfish nature of people. I described a scenario almost everyone would recognize: You're sitting on the highway stuck in bumper-to-bumper traffic. No one is moving and every driver is waiting patiently. Every driver, that is, except one! There's always that indescribably self-centered, egotistical, narcissistic person who selfishly pulls onto the right shoulder and drives past all the other faithful rule followers. I told our church, "That guy will answer to Jesus!" and they all laughed.

The very next day on the way to my church office, the traffic on our two-lane road came to a complete standstill. I was only fifty yards away from the entrance to the church parking lot. After waiting patiently in line for some time with no movement of the cars, it dawned on me that our church owns the land between me and the parking lot entrance. So technically that was kinda-sorta "my land." And, well, if it's my land, I should be able to drive on it, right?

So I did.

I pulled my car over into the grass, which functioned like a shoulder on the road. I passed by a couple of dozen cars and safely pulled into the church parking lot. No harm, no foul, right?

Later that day, a fellow staff member, Mark, told me that he, too, was stuck in the same traffic. While he waited patiently, his ten-year-old son shouted, "Dad, there's one of those selfish guys doing what Pastor Craig talked about, driving on the side of the road!" Then, beside himself, he screamed in disbelief, "Dad, that *is* Pastor Craig!"

Nothing like being busted by a ten-year-old.

We are quick to point fingers and accuse others of hypocrisy. But when we blame our circumstances while shaming someone else's character, isn't that hypocrisy? Doesn't it make us hypocrites too?

I wonder whether we would be less shocked and offended by other people's sin if we were a little more aware and honest about our own.

No surprise that Jesus addressed this problem too. In Luke 6:41–43, he said, "Why do you look at the speck of sawdust in your brother's eye and pay no attention to the plank in your own eye? How can you say to your brother, 'Brother, let me take the speck out of your eye,' when you yourself fail to see the plank in your own eye? You hypocrite, first take the plank out of your eye, and then you will see clearly to remove the speck from your brother's eye."

> I WONDER WHETHER WE WOULD BE LESS SHOCKED AND OFFENDED BY OTHER PEOPLE'S SIN IF WE WERE A LITTLE MORE AWARE AND HONEST ABOUT OUR OWN.

Just like everyone else, and for the same kinds of reasons, we sin. When we do, God doesn't say, in shock, "I can't believe it. How could this happen?!" No, he doesn't flinch, because he knows we are sinners in need of redemption.

He knows we are dust and

- we are weak.
- we give in to temptation.
- we give in to peer pressure.
- we take the easy way out.
- we slip up and say the wrong thing.

Unfortunately, when we sin, we often hurt people.

I hurt people.

You hurt people.

We all do, because we are all the same.

We need to consider how often we suffer from the fundamental attribution error—excusing our sin while exposing others' flaws. If you have been offended by the sin of a Christian, perhaps your expectations were too high. Perhaps you were being judgmental. You forgot that person is dust, just like you.

Shake It Off, Shake It Off (Whoa-Oh-Oh)

In Acts 13, there's a powerful story about Paul and Barnabas. We're told that the word of the Lord spread throughout the whole region where they were doing ministry. God was moving. Good things were happening. Until "the Jewish leaders incited the God-fearing women of high standing and the leading men of the city" (Acts 13:50).

These were the people everyone respected. The "God-fearing women of high standing" were the prayer-warrior ladies. They were the spiritual mothers everyone looked up to. I wonder if they agreed to oppose this move of God because they thought too highly of themselves. And "God-fearing" doesn't necessarily mean Jesus following. I'm not sure, but I do know what they did. "They stirred up persecution against Paul and Barnabas, and expelled them from their region" (v. 50).

These people—who were supposed to represent God—were led astray and drove Paul and Barnabas out of town.

What did Paul and Barnabas do? Did they decide they would leave the faith and no longer meet with believers?

No.

That's not what they did.

They could have, and maybe they would have had they focused only on the offense. But they didn't. They kept on following Jesus and finding other believers they could do life with.

After many years of personal experience, every time I'm hurt by those who claim to follow God, I tell myself this:

A person let me down.

The church didn't let me down.

God didn't let me down.

A bag of dust let me down.

Someone just like me.

So many decide to not go to church anymore when a hypocritical Christian offends them, but that's an emotional response that wars against logic.

We don't do it with restaurants.

Can you imagine getting served bad food at a restaurant and deciding, "That's it. I'm never gonna eat again!"

And you've never proclaimed, "It took almost half an hour to get my burger and fries and they weren't even good, so I am never going to any restaurant again!"

That wouldn't make sense. You wouldn't judge every restaurant on the basis of one restaurant.

Nor should you give up on every church because of a bad experience with one or reject God because of a few Christians who mess up or who may not even actually be Christians.

It's not fair to judge all churches based on one. And it's especially unfair to judge Jesus based on a few of his followers. And it's not fair to you. Because if you lump them all together, call 'em all hypocrites, and just reject everything, it could keep you from Jesus. And that's not fair to you, because you desperately need Jesus. Nothing is worth distancing yourself from him.

So what should you do?

Do what Paul and Barnabas did. They decided, *We're not going to let the sins of some people keep us from the goodness of God. He didn't let us down, people did. And we're all dust.*

What was Paul and Barnabas' next move? "So they shook the dust off their feet as a warning to them and went to Iconium. And the disciples were filled with joy and with the Holy Spirit" (Acts 13:51–52).

Did you notice the word "dust"? They shook it off. They chose joy.

I am not minimizing that you have been hurt. It may have set you back, cost you a lot, robbed you of your innocence, or caused you deep pain. Betrayal sucks. People can be cruel. The pain can be excruciating. But at some point, you'll realize God wants you to heal, move on, and get better.

What do you have to do?

Yep, you have to shake it off too.

I realize that if you've been mistreated, betrayed, or abused, it's going to take a lot of praying, then some shaking, and maybe some counseling, then some shaking, and maybe some more praying and some introspection and some more shaking. It's not easy, but at some point, for your sake, you've got to shake it off. Find the ability to forgive and heal and let it go and, like Paul and Barnabas, move on filled with the joy of the Holy Spirit.

Please know I don't say any of that lightly. I find that I've got to shake things off every week. I understand the biggest complaint against the church may be that it's full of narrow-minded, judgmental hypocrites. I don't want that to be true, but the greatest hurts I have experienced personally have been from churchgoing, narrow-minded, judgmental hypocrites.

So I get it.

And I want to say this to you: If you've been hurt by the church, or a hypocrite who goes to one, I am sorry. I'm sorry because church people do not always get it right.

Some in the church say one thing and then do another.

Some church leaders have abused their power.

Some Christians can be arrogant, harsh, unkind, and unloving.

It is ugly. And that's not Jesus. It does not honor God. There is no excuse, and I am sorry.

Sincerely. I am sorry someone claiming to be a Christian hurt you.

Full transparency: Even as a pastor, the truth is that I sometimes lose my temper or slip into pride. I can be critical. I can focus more on being right than being loving. When I do, I hurt people, and I am sorry.

But can I ask you something? If you've been hurt by people and it led you to lose your faith in Jesus, is it possible your faith was in people when it should have been in Jesus?

Could you ask God to help you see whether this might be true for you?

Are you potentially struggling with your faith in Jesus, not because of Jesus, but because you put your faith in a fallible person instead of our sinless Savior?

Can I encourage you to look to Jesus, because he will never let you down?

People will. Jesus won't.

Read the Gospels and look at his life.

Not the hypocrites, not the people, just Jesus.

Look at how he lived and loved.

Look at how he confronted hypocrisy.

Look at how he showed compassion for the least, the last, and the lost.

Look at how he defended the abused and the oppressed, the widows and the poor.

Look at how people who were turned off by religion were drawn to Jesus.

Look at how people who were sinful or broken wanted to be around him, because he wanted to be around them.

Can I encourage you to look to Jesus and shake off whatever people have done to you? After all, they're just dust.

IF YOU'VE BEEN HURT BY PEOPLE AND IT LED YOU TO LOSE YOUR FAITH IN JESUS, IS IT POSSIBLE YOUR FAITH WAS IN PEOPLE WHEN IT SHOULD HAVE BEEN IN JESUS?

You may think, *Well, Craig, that's easy for you to say.*

But it's not.

Remember that my sister was sexually abused, for years, by a man who, the whole time, taught Sunday school at our church? That man never apologized, and he continued to claim he was a Christian his whole life.

What did we do?

Our family—led by my sister—decided to forgive him.

That was not easy. Choosing to forgive what felt unforgivable may have been one of the most difficult things our family has ever done. It was a Spirit-led journey that took a lot of years and a lot of shaking. It took counseling and praying. But ultimately God helped us to shake off the dust.

We wrote him a letter explaining why we forgave him and shared the gospel with him.

It turns out that when he received it, he was on his deathbed. His hospice nurse read him our letter. We learned later that both he and the nurse were very moved, and that the two of them prayed together.

Honestly, I don't know what happened to him in that moment, but I do know what happened to our family.

My sister, by the grace of God, let it go.

We shook it off.

We were not going to let the sin of a person keep us from living in the goodness of God.

We were not going to let his hypocrisy keep us from living in the grace and forgiveness of Jesus.

And we were not going to let the pain he caused keep us from living in the joy of the Holy Spirit.

I know it's not easy. But if you've been hurt by someone who claimed to be a Christian, shake it off and look to Jesus.

Trust in him.

Rest in him.

Put your whole faith in him.

Jesus will never let you down.

> **Jesus looked at them and said, "With man this is impossible, but with God all things are possible."**
> **—Matthew 19:26**

CHAPTER 6 EXERCISE

1. Like Chloe's, Brian's, and my sister's stories in this chapter, have you ever had a toxic experience with a Christian you trusted? Explain.

2. How is it "false advertising" when there is a difference between the life of Jesus and the lives of those who claim to follow him?

3. Why do you think Jesus so directly addressed the hypocrisy of the Pharisees? How can we apply his rebuke to our lives today?

4. Do you suppose there are ways that our culture breeds people who seem to mistakenly believe they are Christians? Explain.

5. How might the section "Maybe They're Just Baby Christians" help you better understand and allow for varying levels of spiritual maturity in your brothers and sisters in Christ?

6. How might accepting that we are all "imperfect, in-process Christians" help you grow in God's grace, forgiveness, reconciliation, and a sense of community?

7. On a scale of 1 (not at all) to 10 (all the time), how would you rate your struggle with the fundamental attribution error—excusing our own sin while exposing others' sin? Explain.

8. What are your thoughts on Jesus' teaching about the speck and the plank in Luke 6:41–43? How might this teaching affect your being offended by or judging others?

9. What are some ways you can apply Paul and Barnabas' response to the God-fearing people who drove them out of town in Acts 13?

10. Is there a person or circumstance in your life that this chapter has helped you see that you need to forgive, let go of, and shake off—for your sake? Explain.

CHAPTER 7

Why Does God Feel So Far Away?

At just sixteen years old, Megan couldn't hold back the tears as she told me her story one Sunday after church. She loved her mother, who wasn't a believer, but that along with a dozen other reasons kept them from being close. Her dad was the one who "got her" and made her feel safe and loved during those turbulent teen years. He had always been strong, emotionally available, and present. But after a nine-month battle with a brain tumor, Megan's dad was gone. And so was her joy.

With nowhere else to turn, every Sunday, Megan would drive herself to church hoping to experience God's presence and his promised peace. But every Sunday, she left disappointed. As much as she sought after and needed God, she just couldn't seem to find him.

Megan confided in me, "I see other people and, like, they lift their hands in worship and they're crying, and so they're obviously feeling something, but," she hesitated, trying to find the words, "I don't feel any-thing . . . but numb.

"I read my Bible," she continued, "but it doesn't always make a lot of sense to me. And when I pray, well, I want to believe God is there, but I don't really feel anything even then. I beg him for peace, but it seems like he either doesn't care or he's gone, just like my dad."

My heart ached for Megan as she confessed, "I want to believe, but I don't feel *anything*. I want to believe God is with me, but it's hard for me to sense his presence."

Can you relate to Megan?

I can.

Have you ever felt like her?

I have.

I have a long history of feeling as though God is absent when he promised to be present.

Such as my first Communion in the Methodist church where I was raised. When I was twelve years old, I went through the confirmation class, at the end of which we all got to take Communion. They told me, "It will be the holiest moment of your life. You will taste the body and blood of Christ. Your sins will be forgiven. You are going to experience the powerful and unforgettable presence of God!"

The day came and I knelt at the altar with spiritual anticipation. As the pastor approached, I could barely contain my expectancy. "Take and eat," he said solemnly, handing me a dry wafer that reminded me of eating a baseball card, *not* the body of Christ. But I knew what was next—the wine! It would be my first sip of alcohol (and completely legal because it was *holy* alcohol). "Take and drink," the pastor said as my excitement rose. But, no, it was grape juice. *What? Ugh.* My first Holy Communion and I felt nothing. Not only was the experience a letdown but it left a bad taste in my mouth.

Another time was a few months after marrying Amy. I was invited to a men's spiritual retreat. My friends said it was *The. Best. Thing. Ever.* "Craig, this is the closest thing to being in heaven." So I decided to leave Amy (which was annoying, because being with her was the closest thing to heaven for me) to spend a weekend in almost-heaven with a bunch of dudes. But the truth is the retreat felt more like hell. Just a bunch of smelly guys in a smelly gym. Though most of them seemed to love it, I hated every minute and wondered what was wrong with me. My friends said it was the closest they ever felt to God, yet I felt nothing.

What were they experiencing?

What was I missing?

And then there was my ordination. To become a pastor, I studied four years in seminary while working full-time to get my master of divinity degree. The first time I was up for ordination, I was rejected. (A story I shared in more detail in *Think Ahead*.) After transferring denominations, I had to do *another* twenty-one semester hours of school and then go through a probationary period. Finally, after *more than ten years* of preparation, I was given permission to be ordained. Even though I had to fly to another state for the ceremony, I was confident this would be something special and memorable. It was, but not for the reasons I'd hoped. I will never forget my ordination because I had the worst case of diarrhea ever. I was by the altar in my ordination robe, just trying to hold it in. Pastors were praying; I was pinching. They kept praying. I kept pinching. I did feel something that day, but, trust me, it was not the Holy Spirit.

What do you do when you desperately want to feel the presence of God but don't?

What if you're seeking God, but he still seems really far away?

What if you begin to doubt whether he's there at all?

[Not] Feeling God's Presence

There are some questions I wrestle with about the presence of God. I'd like to ask you to join me in grappling with them. Ready?

Do you believe you've felt the presence of God at some point? A time when you just knew he was there with you? You had a moment when you related to David's words, "I know the LORD is always with me. I will not be shaken, for he is right beside me. No wonder my heart is glad, and I rejoice. . . . You will show me the way of life, granting me the joy of your presence and the pleasures of living with you forever" (Ps. 16:8–9, 11 NLT).

Have you ever felt God's presence like that?

If not, stick with me as we dive in.

If so, here's a follow-up question: How did you know? How do you know you felt God and it wasn't just your emotions playing tricks on you?

Maybe you had a tingling sensation? Or perhaps you were so over-whelmed with emotion that you cried? Or you felt an unusual heavenly peace that transcended the chaotic circumstances you were experiencing?

Is that how you knew you were in the presence of God?

Because his presence can give you a tingly feeling, right? Well, so can test-driving a new car or taking the first bite of an incredible dessert or hearing that you're about to get a big raise. Is it God or an endorphin rush?

God's presence can make you cry tears of joy, but so can a really touch-ing YouTube video or the end of all six *Rocky* movies.

God's presence is incredibly peaceful, but so is drinking chamomile tea in a bubble bath surrounded by a bunch of flickering pumpkin-spice-scented candles. (Or so I've heard.)

So if you think you've experienced God's presence, how can you be sure?

Here's another challenging question: When you don't feel the pres-ence of God, whose fault is it? Is it his fault? Is he holding out on you? Or is it your fault? Perhaps God wanted to show up in a palpable, powerful way, but you weren't paying attention. Could it be you did something wrong? Or if it wasn't God's fault or yours, maybe it was someone else's? Perhaps it was your kids being so loud when you were trying to pray. Or maybe the problem was the worship pastor because he didn't pick any of your favorite songs at church—again.

If you didn't feel God's presence, whose fault is it?

What do you do when you want to feel the presence of God but don't?

Is there anything you can do?

IF YOU'RE WONDERING WHETHER GOD IS WITH YOU, DON'T PANIC. YOU ARE NOT ALONE.

If you struggle with these ques-tions, or if you're wondering whether God is with you, don't panic. You are not alone.

You Aren't Alone in Not Feeling God's Presence

"Why, Lord, are you far from me?"

"Why do you reject me?"

"Why have you forsaken me?"

These are words you may have thought or prayed but not dared to speak out loud. You may have felt embarrassed by these questions or wondered what they say about you and your relationship with God. Well, here's some good news. Several heroes in the Bible, who were some of God's most faithful servants, uttered these exact words, including his very own Son.

David was called a man after God's own heart (Acts 13:22). He probably spoke about feeling God's presence more than anyone else in the Bible. Yet he wrote, "I cry to you for help, LORD; in the morning my prayer comes before you. Why, LORD, do you reject me and hide your face from me?" (Ps. 88:13–14).

That wasn't just an anomaly. In many of the psalms that David wrote for the congregation to sing together, he expressed a feeling of being abandoned by God. For instance, "How long, LORD? Will you forget me forever? How long will you hide your face from me?" (Ps. 13:1) and "You have rejected us, God" (Ps. 60:1) and "Why are you so far from saving me, so far from my cries of anguish? My God, I cry out by day, but you do not answer, by night, but I find no rest" (Ps. 22:1–2).

Imagine the worship leader at your church displaying any of these words on the screen next Sunday and asking everyone to sing along. What if he or she calls out, "C'mon, church! Lift your voices and join me. 'You have rejected us, God!'" Kind of puts David's bold honesty in perspective, huh?

If you've ever felt a strange absence of God's presence, if you've cried out for God to speak but heard nothing in return, you are not alone. David understood.

You know who else does? Jesus. No one was closer to God than Jesus. In John 10:30, he says, "The Father and I are one" (NLT). The two walked intimately together every day of Jesus' life on earth. His mission was to glorify God in every way, and he was obedient even to death. On the cross,

Jesus was insulted and mocked. On the cross, Jesus became sin for us. And, on the cross, in some mysterious way, God pulled back or looked away—because he is too holy to look on sin—and Jesus' soul was flooded with all our sin.

While this is very difficult for us to understand, here's what I do know: Jesus, the Son of God, who had done nothing but his Father's will, cried out in desperate agony, "My God, my God, why have you forsaken me?" (Matt. 27:46).

This is one of the many reasons that Hebrews 4:15 says of Jesus, "We do not have a high priest who is unable to empathize with our weaknesses."

If you've ever wondered why you don't feel the presence of God, you are not alone. Jesus understands.

Why Don't We Always Feel God?

When I was in high school, even though I wasn't sure whether God existed, I went to a spiritual retreat. (Why? Because I was invited. And thought there might be cute girls there.) (Also because I was hurting and hoping God was real.) (But truthfully it was mostly about the girls.) At one point they told us, "Go have a quiet time with God."

So I wandered into a field and sat underneath a towering shade tree. On the ground, I saw some small sticks (or big twigs—I'm not sure how best to describe them. I was not quite an atheist, and definitely not an arborist). Desperate to hear from God, I took the two twiggy sticks and placed them in the form of a cross. I thought I was doing something spiritual for God, then I challenged him to do something spiritual for me. Generously, I gave him a wide berth, asking, "God, do something to these sticks. Anything. Anything at all. Your choice. Fire from heaven would be amazing. Or you could just move one of them. Or an earthquake. A bird swooping in to pick one up would be super cool. I'll take a big south wind. Or an angel from heaven. However you want. Just do something with one of these sticks and I will serve you forever. I need to feel something, to see something. I just want to know you're real."

You may not be as creative with kindling as I am, but you've probably been desperate for God to reveal himself to you in some way.

Maybe you're trying to make a decision about someone you're dating and praying, "Should I stay in this? Or break up and believe for someone better?" You want an audible response, like "Thou shalt breaketh up witheth himeth because an upgradeth cometh."

Or you want to know whether you should change jobs and you've been begging God for an answer. Or you're considering a move across the country and want some kind of confirmation whether it's a good idea or a bad idea. Or you have two kids but want to know whether you should try for a third.

It may not be about a decision at all. You might be hurting and just want to experience God's peace in the pain. Or you feel alone and want to know that he is with you.

So if God is always there, and he always loves us, why don't we always feel him?

Let's consider three possible reasons.

Reason 1: You Might Sensationalize God's Presence

Perhaps you're looking for an awe-inspiring, supernatural manna from heaven, water from a rock, parting of the sea, closed mouths of hungry lions, walk through fire unharmed experience with God. Yes, that *is* possible, but it's not always the way we encounter God. It may be rare, and that may be a good thing.

On one occasion, the Pharisees and Sadducees came asking for Jesus to show them a sign proving God was present with him. Jesus responded, "A wicked and adulterous generation looks for a sign, but none will be given it except the sign of Jonah" (Matt. 16:4). The "sign of Jonah" was that Jesus would walk out of his grave three days after being buried. He was telling them that his resurrection was all they really needed.

If you wonder, *What's wrong with me? Why don't I feel the presence of God?* I want you to know that feelings are not the only evidence of his presence.

That's part of what Jesus was communicating to the religious leaders in Matthew 16.

If you always felt God, you wouldn't need faith.

If you always trusted your feelings, I'm guessing you'd be in jail right now. I know I would.

> **IF YOU ALWAYS FELT GOD, YOU WOULDN'T NEED FAITH.**

Feelings are not the only evidence of the presence of God. He's way better, way bigger, and way broader than what we feel.

For example, my job is about as spiritual as you can get. Because I'm a pastor, my entire life is centered around God, Jesus, and the Holy Spirit, and praying, sharing the gospel, and serving people. Yet I have been in ministry for more than thirty years and have had maybe ten supernatural experiences of God that left me awestruck.

I don't think that's the way the Christian life usually works, and I'm glad for that. Why? Because not only does it lead me to live by faith instead of feelings but also it means I have a more mature relationship with God. It's like my relationship with Amy. When we first met and fell in love, there were lots of fluttery, bubbly feelings. There was a lot of "You're my smoopie bear." "No, you're *my* smoopie bear." "I love you to the moon and back." "Well, I love you to infinity and beyond." But there was also a lot of insecurity. I wasn't sure how she felt about me. I needed proof of her love. I wanted demonstrations of her commitment. That was understandable because we were new to each other and there was a lot of uncertainty.

Today, I am so thankful I don't require that kind of validation anymore. While, of course, there are still feelings, I don't need feelings to be assured of our commitment. Our love is deeper than that now and more mature. We can sit quietly in a room together not always having to check in with each other, totally comfortable and completely happy, without hype and smoopie bears and the moon.

That's the kind of relationship I want with God.

If you don't feel as though you're experiencing the presence of God, maybe you're sensationalizing it.

Maybe you're relying on feelings more than faith.

Maybe you need to focus less on the insecurity in your faith and more on gaining maturity for your faith.

Here's a promise about his presence in Colossians 1:22: "Yet now he has reconciled you to himself through the death of Christ in his physical body. As a result, he has brought you into his own presence, and you are holy and blameless as you stand before him without a single fault" (NLT).

You might be looking for proof when it's not necessary. Jesus has already displayed his unconditional love when he gave his life for you on the cross.

Reason 2: You Might Have a Hard Heart

I just told you that Amy and I don't need supercharged feelings to be sure of each other's love.

Not *needing* feelings can be a sign of a mature relationship.

Not *having* feelings can be a sign of a marriage that's in trouble.

It can be the result of a spouse who has pulled away and become distant in the relationship.

In a similar way, some people don't experience God because their hearts have hardened. Jesus described this when he quoted Isaiah, "You will be ever hearing but never understanding; you will be ever seeing but never perceiving. For this people's heart has become calloused; they hardly hear with their ears, and they have closed their eyes" (Matt. 13:14–15).

If you're wondering why you don't experience the presence of God or why you don't sense he's with you, you might be a Christian who has allowed your heart to harden.

Just as when one spouse starts to become distant in the marriage, our hearts don't normally turn hard overnight. It happens slowly, and often without our even knowing, at least at first.

How does a heart become hardened?

Bitterness

Someone does something to hurt you and you slowly close off your heart to people and then eventually to God. Or you ask God to do something but he doesn't provide or respond the way you thought he would, and you feel crushing disappointment. In time, you conclude, "I can't really trust God" and your heart begins to harden. This is why we're warned, "See to it that no one falls short of the grace of God and that no bitter root grows up" (Heb. 12:15). In Paul's "get rid of" list of sins in Ephesians 4:31, bitterness is first, even before rage, anger, brawling, slander, and malice.

A heart can also become hardened by sinfulness.

Sinfulness

I'm referring not to a one-time spiritual misstep but to ongoing sin that you allow to continue in your life. You're not warring against it. You're not confessing it. You've accepted, rationalized, and tolerated it. So, over time, your heart becomes covered in sin that will keep you from feeling and enjoying God's presence.

For example, imagine it's winter and bitter cold outside. It's all-your-nose-hairs-freeze-as-soon-as-you-walk-out-the-door weather. What do you do? You bundle up! You put on your long underwear and a sweater and your thickest coat and gloves and hat and scarf. (You look like Ralphie's brother in *A Christmas Story*: "I can't put my arms down!") You walk out of the house covered in clothes so you can't feel the cold. Your layers separate you from the frigid air to keep you warm.

While layers of clothes separate you from harmful elements, layers of sin separate you from what you desperately need. Ongoing sin prevents us from feeling the warmth of God's love, leaving our hearts out in the cold. Our sin separates us from God. Not his love but his presence.

I'll ask you the same question I ask myself when God feels far away: Is there a sin with which you've gotten comfortable? One that you've found a way to rationalize because you've made friends with it and don't want to give it up?

Sins such as these:

- **JEALOUSY.** You're envious of anyone who has perfect hair and perfect kids and more shoes than a Kardashian.

- **ANGER.** When someone says or does something that annoys or offends you, you let everyone know by your irritated attitude and words.
- **LUST.** You look and lust and look and lust and look and lust. You tell yourself, "Well, at least I'm not doing something worse." But you know the truth, which is that you're caught in a prison you cannot escape.

We live in a culture that has made sin into entertainment. It's everywhere and it's accepted. Perhaps you've bought into the lie that your sin is okay. You justify it, make excuses for it, and accept it as a part of who you are and what you do. We have to watch out for the warning signs—what we tell ourselves or others when we rationalize sin, such as, "Oh, you know me. That's just how I roll," or, "What's it going to hurt? People are guilty of this every day."

How else does a heart harden?

Reason 3: You Might Prioritize Performance

Instead of living *from* God's grace and approval, we try to live *for* it.

For example, when I first became a Christian, I knew I had to stop doing all the "big sins." I stopped getting drunk, having sex, and cursing like someone on *Breaking Bad* or *The Wire*.

After getting rid of those, I was on fire for God and wanted to start taking new steps forward. I got obsessed with Bible study and prayer and attending church and listening to Christian radio and wearing (often obnoxious) T-shirts like the one that said, "I took a DNA test and God is my Father."

Along the way, I realized I wasn't really experiencing the presence of God. Why? There wasn't an issue of ongoing unconfessed sin. No, something more subtle and insidious was happening. My life had become more about my performance than about God's presence. There had been a subtle shift from living in genuine devotion to God to doing religious duties for God. I was relying on my "D-O" instead of Jesus' "D-O-N-E."

Rather than living my life *with* God, I was living my life *for* God. No won-der it didn't feel as though he was with me as much as before. It was all about me and had almost nothing to do with him. (Remember when we talked about deconstruction? This was one of the reasons people gave for eventually losing their faith.)

So how about you?

Why don't you feel God's presence?

Could it be that you are sensationalizing his presence?

Or that you've allowed your heart to grow hard and cold to the things of God?

Or are you rationalizing a sin?

Or are you struggling with prioritizing your performance over God's presence?

God Might Be Drawing You Close

As a dad to half a dozen kids, I've noticed something. Once they get to a certain age, it's very easy for them to become self-reliant and pretty much ignore their parents. Now that I'm an empty nester with grown and married kids, I find that they show up when they need money, when they need a babysitter, or occasionally when they feel alone or desperate and want advice.

God wants you to stay close to him and live dependent on him. But it's tempting for us to keep our distance and live independently—that is, until we realize we need him. Because of that, God will lead you to seek him.

God does not need anything, but his creation always needs him. Paul told the people at the Areopagus in Athens, "God did this so that they would seek him and perhaps reach out for him and find him, though he is not far from any one of us" (Acts 17:27).

Paul said that God is not far from any of us. The problem is we may be far from him.

God wants you to seek him, reach out to him, and find him. So perhaps he's let you get to a point where you crave him. You may feel alone, and that will cause you to seek him. You're feeling desperate, so you finally realize that you need him.

One of the most meaningful attributes of God is that he is relational and wants to be pursued. He is a loving and intimate God who wants your heart and devotion.

Think about this: When you are deprived of something, what happens?

When you don't eat, you get hungry and so you eat.

When you don't drink, you get thirsty and so you drink.

And when you don't feel God's presence? You're awakened to how insufficient and bankrupt you are without him. You understand that you need him every moment to meet every need. You long for him. You hunger and thirst for him. So you seek him. And, if you do, you will find him. God made that promise in Jeremiah 29:13: "You will seek me and find me when you seek me with all your heart."

So if God seems far away, remind yourself that just because he feels distant, it doesn't mean he is absent. Your feelings are not facts and can fool you.

He *is* there.

He is *close*.

And he's trying to draw you close.

He's not far from you.

If you seek him, just as he has invited you to do, you may experience his presence in a way that brings tears to your eyes and gives you goose bumps. Occasionally. Probably just occasionally. At least that's the way my life goes. I tend to experience God most in the quietness of ordinary, everyday, simple moments.

In 1 Kings 19:1–18, there's a story about Elijah the prophet. When his life was threatened, he ran away to the wilderness and ended up at Mount Horeb. After he spent the night in a cave, "the word of the LORD came to him: 'What are you doing here, Elijah?'" (v. 9). He explained his dilemma, then "the LORD said, 'Go out and stand on the mountain in the presence of the LORD, for the LORD is about to pass by'" (v. 11). A powerful wind tore through the area, but God was not in it. Next, an earthquake struck, but God was not in it. Then a fire swept through, but God was not in it.

Wouldn't you expect God to be in at least one of these powerful displays of nature? What happened next is the real surprise.

"And after the fire came a gentle whisper" (v. 12).

When Elijah heard the voice, he went outside the cave and God spoke again. We aren't told how Elijah knew that God wasn't in the wind, earthquake, and fire, but somehow the prophet knew that the whisper was God. Had he heard it before? Did he recognize more where God was than wasn't?

When I was a kid at the retreat and I wanted God to show me some display of his power, I asked him to do something to those two twigs. Don't we often want something big and dramatic so we can be sure he is there? Something tangible we can see or hear or feel that wouldn't require us to trust him and have faith?

Yes, there will be times in our lives when he speaks and moves and works in incredible ways, but, most often, he seems to want us to follow his advice in Psalm 46:10: "Be still, and know that I am God."

Listen for his whisper, perhaps during times like these:

- You open the Bible App from YouVersion and the Verse of the Day is just what you needed.
- You're having one of "those days" and your friend reaches out to check on you.
- You're feeling spiritually dry and your kid surprises you with a faith-filled prayer.
- You hear a song and it feels as if the lyrics were written just for you.
- You barely make it to church and then find that the sermon is exactly the encouragement you needed.

And so you realize, again, that God *is* with you. He is always with you; he will never leave or forsake you.

> **GOD IS ALWAYS WITH YOU AND WILL NEVER LEAVE OR FORSAKE YOU.**

- When you don't know what to do, he is with you as your guide (John 16:13).
- When you are hurting, he is with you as your comforter (Jer. 8:18; John 14:16).
- When you feel all alone, he is with you as a friend who sticks closer than a brother (Prov. 18:24).
- When you're overwhelmed with anxiety, he is with you as a heavenly peace that goes beyond your ability to understand (Phil. 4:7).
- When you sin, he is with you as your Savior (1 John 1:9).
- Be near to God. Make him your refuge (Ps. 73:28).
- Before you take on anything important, ask him for help (Ps. 124:8).
- When you're worried about someone you love, cast your cares on him (1 Peter 5:7).
- When you're troubled, cry out to Jesus (Ps. 34:17).

Do You Recognize Him?

Remember Megan? The sixteen-year-old girl I was talking to in the lobby after church who told me her father died? With tears in her eyes, she asked me, "Where is God? I just can't feel him."

While I could see and hear her pain, at the same time I saw something special in this girl. It was so obvious. She was serious about seeking God, driving herself to church every week, despite her doubts and no support from her family, and coming to talk it out with me rather than burying her doubts and holding them in.

I tried to encourage her. "God loves you so much. And he is with you.

He's always been with you. I promise you're going to experience his presence. I promise, because I can see you are stubborn in a good way."

Normally I wouldn't have called someone that I barely knew "stubborn." Yet for some reason those words just came out of my mouth, almost without thinking. As I said it, I hoped she wouldn't be offended. But the moment I said "stubborn in a good way," her face instantly changed. She asked soberly, "What did you just say?"

I was afraid I had offended her, but I repeated, "You're stubborn in a *good* way," emphasizing the word *good*.

"I can't believe you just said that," she told me with now happy tears streaming down her cheeks. "My daddy used to always say that. He would tell me I was his 'stubborn little angel.' That was his nickname for me. He called me that since I was a little girl. I can't believe you just said, I'm 'stubborn in a good way.'"

I was blown away and asked, while clearly seeing the holiness of the moment, "Do you recognize him? Do you realize that God is here, close, that he is with you right now?"

She gave me a knowing smile and nodded. "Yes, I do," she said, wiping tears from her eyes. It was obvious to both of us. She had been seeking God. And she found him. Megan didn't say it, but I'm guessing she may have felt some goose bumps in that moment when God had me say what her daddy would call her.

Why?

Because I think God was revealing his presence to Megan.

Why?

Because she was seeking him.

So now it's your time.

Seek him.

Call on him.

Cry out to him.

Cry out in your pain, in your fears, in your hurt, and in your desperation.

If you seek him, you'll find him.

He might feel far away, but he is not far from you.

> But as for me, it is good to be near God.
> —Psalm 73:28

CHAPTER 7 EXERCISE

1. Think about Megan's story and my own. Have you ever had a similar experience where you wanted to feel God's presence but couldn't? Explain.
2. Can you relate to David in the Psalms as he cries out to God for answers? How do you feel about the blunt honesty of his words?
3. Why do you think we tend to want signs and big displays from God to prove or confirm his presence?
4. When was the last time there was a situation or decision in your life for which you were praying for God's help but you felt as though he was not present? Explain.
5. What are your thoughts on the statement "If you always felt God, you wouldn't need faith"?
6. How can relying more on faith rather than feelings help us become more mature and secure in our relationship with God?
7. Do you feel you have ever sensationalized God's presence in any aspect of your life? Explain.
8. Has bitterness or sinfulness ever kept you from experiencing God's presence? Explain.
9. Have you ever struggled with prioritizing your performance over God's presence? Explain.
10. After reading the sections "God Might Be Drawing You Close" and "Do You Recognize Him?" do you have a better understanding of God's presence? Explain.

Why Would God Send People to Hell?

I think we all agree that it's better if we don't talk about it.

Hell, that is.

Just don't mention it. In fact, as a kid, I was taught to not even say the word. I had to say "H-E-double-hockey-sticks" instead.

It was such a forbidden topic that I felt like a rebel (who might go to hell) when I typed 7-7-3-4 on my calculator at school, then turned it upside down to show my friends. (To save you the trouble, I just tried it on my phone calculator and it doesn't really work.)

Today, the word *hell* is used a little more loosely. You might even hear someone at church lament that "the world is going to hell in a handbasket." (BTW: What exactly is a handbasket? Is it one of those plastic things you grab at the grocery store when you need only a few items? And why is a handbasket the primary mode of transportation for items sent to hell?)

Even though I wasn't supposed to say the *h* word when I was a kid, I was still *very* afraid of going to hell. I'd lie in bed feeling guilty for all the things I'd done wrong during the day and pray "God, don't send me to hell, don't send me to hell, don't send me to hell" until I fell asleep. Then I might wake up and realize I hadn't signed off. I hadn't ended my prayer

with a "Ten-four, good buddy," or "Sincerely, Craig," or God's favorite pleas-
antry: "Amen."

It would hit me that if I had "died before I wake" instead of "the Lord
my soul to take," I would have likely gone to hell because I hadn't completed
my prayer properly! So I would re-pray my previous night's prayer, "God,
don't send me to hell, don't send me to hell, don't send me to hell," then
give God a bunch of extra amens. "Amen, amen, amen—those were for
last night. Amen, amen, amen—for tonight. Amen, amen, amen—in case
I forget tomorrow night. Amen, amen, amen—extras!"

My point? I was *really* afraid of hell.

But aren't most people?

Hell is confusing to many people and often cultivates disturbing
doubts that lead to the big question: "Why would a loving God send anyone to a horrible place like hell?"

It's especially troublesome because it's not just a philosophical
question, it's a personal one. Thinking not only about why God might
send someone there but also about who might go there is agonizing, so
most people dismiss the topic altogether. But that is a really big gamble.
Wouldn't you agree? It seems irresponsible to not think about what might
happen to us and the people we love after we die.

But I get it, hell is so uncomfortable to think about.

Maybe that's why everyone seems to agree: it's better if we just don't
talk about it.

On the subject of hell, C. S. Lewis said, "There is no doctrine which
I would more willingly remove from Christianity than this if it lay in my
power. But it has the full support of Scripture and, specifically, of our
Lord's own words."[1]

He's right, *Jesus* talked about it. Quite a bit. That brings up another
question: Why would loving and gentle Jesus talk about an evil place
like hell?

I think it's important for us to talk about hell so we can understand it
and hopefully alleviate our doubts about whether God might send people
there.

But for us to understand hell, it will be helpful for us to first talk about heaven. You might think, *That's a good idea, because heaven is an easier topic that we can all feel good about and agree on.*

Well, actually, you may be surprised. Feel good about? Yes. Agree on? Not necessarily.

What Is Heaven?

People tend to think heaven will be filled with whatever they want it to be filled with.

For the ladies:

- You get to live in a Pinterest-perfect mansion!
- You're on an endless, all-inclusive beach vacation!
- Instead of driving your kids around like an unpaid Uber driver, you are chauffeured around in a blinged-out limo!
- Your husband brings you flowers and reads you romantic poetry as he cooks dinner each night!
- And calorie-free chocolate truffles!

Or for the guys:

- You're served endless medium-rare rib eyes, covered in butter!
- Your team always wins the Super Bowl—and you're the quarterback!
- You drive a Lamborghini!
- You are amazingly good looking and in perfect shape for all eternity!
- And endless Flamin' Hot Cheetos! (Actually, they might fit better in hell, but you get my point.)

We assume heaven will be like a never-ending party or vacation with all the perks. It's an idea pastor John Ortberg calls "the eternal pleasure factory."[2] Who wouldn't want that? We all would, and so the assumption is that everyone would want to go to this version of heaven.

But do you know where we get those ideas about heaven?

We made them up!

People believe heaven will be like that because people want heaven to be like that. Not only is that inaccurate but it's also insane.

My family has vacationed in Steamboat Springs, Colorado. If I told you that the mountains there are made of gumdrops, the snow is white chocolate, and everyone you meet will give you a hundred-dollar bill just for being you, that would sound amazing. But Steamboat Springs is a real place, so I can't make up what it's like. Heaven is a real place, so we can't make up what it's like either.

So what is heaven actually like?

Heaven is life with God.

God created human beings to be with him, to know him intimately and experience life with him eternally. But we sin, and our sin interferes with life with God. So Jesus came to earth and died for our sins so we might have life with God—before we die *and* after. The Bible teaches that death is not an end for us. It's a doorway to a new and forever kind of life. Here's how the Bible describes heaven: "Look! God's dwelling place is now among the people, and he will dwell with them. They will be his people, and God himself will be with them and be their God" (Rev. 21:3).

Did you see it? God "will dwell with them." Heaven is not the eternal pleasure factory. Heaven is life with God.

I like the way Ortberg explains it: "Heaven does not contain God; God contains heaven."[3]

HEAVEN IS NOT THE ETERNAL PLEASURE FACTORY. HEAVEN IS LIFE WITH GOD.

We think heaven is this great big amusement park, and somewhere in it—maybe in the middle, because he is pretty important—God will be sitting on a throne. So if you ever want to be with God, you can just go to the throne. (Kind of like going to see Mickey at Disney.)

No.

Look at this picture we get of heaven in the Bible: "I did not see a temple in the city, because the Lord God Almighty and the Lamb are its temple. The city does not need the sun or the moon to shine on it, for the glory of God gives it light, and the Lamb is its lamp" (Rev. 21:22–23).

In heaven, God is everywhere.

Heaven does not contain God. God contains heaven.

No matter where you go or what you do, you will not be able to avoid God in heaven.

That means if you're not the kind of person who wants to be with God, heaven is not the kind of place you'd enjoy. Or if you're the kind of person who wants to keep sinning, heaven is the kind of place that would make you uncomfortable.

If you find yourself sinning in this life but desperately don't want to, heaven is going to solve that problem.

But if you enjoy and want to continue sinning, and want to keep your sin a secret, even from God, heaven would be a problem for you. Because there will be no place where God is not.

Heaven is eternal, uninterrupted life with God.

People who want to be with God will love it.

People who would rather avoid God would never want to go.

What Is Hell?

Now that we have a more accurate understanding of heaven, we can better answer this question: What is hell?

The Bible says that hell is real. One reason some doubt the reality of hell is because the word brings to mind cartoonish images of torture-chamber dungeons ruled by a long-tailed, pitchfork-carrying red devil. That's not what the Bible says about hell. I wonder whether we get those ideas about hell from the devil. The most strategic thing that Satan could do is attempt to convince everyone that hell is not real, or not something to be taken seriously. Then there's also the other side of that coin, where people believe hell is a never-ending party where you can do anything you please with no consequences. All of these beliefs make it easier for people to reject Christ and live a sin-justifying, self-centered, comfort-craving, sacrifice-rejecting, persecution-avoiding life, spent loving a world that will not last.

That's what most people do. Jesus warned us about this in Matthew 7:13–14 when he said, "You can enter God's Kingdom only through the narrow gate. The highway to hell is broad, and its gate is wide for the many who choose that way. But the gateway to life is very narrow and the road is difficult, and only a few ever find it" (NLT).

But why? Why is that highway broad and the gate wide?

Part of it is because people don't believe in hell. It's easy not to believe in, especially since we don't talk about it.

Except Jesus did.

The subject of hell comes up quite a bit in the Bible, and Jesus talked about it more than anyone. That's confusing to many people because Jesus was the most compassionate person ever. But that's exactly why he spoke of hell so often. *Because* he was compassionate. Because he *is* love, he didn't want anyone to go there.

Max Lucado teaches, "Jesus Christ positioned himself on the cross as if to say, 'If you want to go to hell, you've got to go through me.' That's how much I love you."[4]

Jesus once gave an outrageous metaphor to warn people about the danger of going to hell when he said that if your right eye causes you to stumble, gouge it out and throw it away. If you ever struggle with lust, just rip that eye out. I'm picturing a men's group full of guys all walking in with eye patches! Jesus said, "Gouge it out and throw it away. It is better for you to lose one part of your body than for your whole body to be thrown into hell" (Matt. 5:29).

Jesus knew hell was real and wanted the threat to be understood for us to avoid it at any cost.

The word Jesus used for hell in Matthew 5 is translated from the Greek word *Gehenna*, which was an actual place in the southwest corner of the city of Jerusalem.

This area was known as the Valley of Hinnom. Centuries before Jesus, the evil king Ahaz worshiped the false god Molech with child sacrifices.

We read in Jeremiah 7:31 that a "high place" was built in the Valley of Hinnom where moms and dads could burn their sons and daughters to death as sacrifices to Molech. If you go to Jerusalem today, you will not find homes or businesses in Gehenna because it's always been considered cursed and cut off from God.

Because of its evil history, Gehenna became a despised garbage dump where the people would throw dead animals, human waste, sewage, and the bodies of executed criminals. The waste was burned with a smoldering fire and the whole area had a putrid smell.

We could refer to this valley as "the land of no more."

- No more beauty.
- No more laughter.
- No more peace.
- No more friendship.
- No more joy.
- No more hope.
- No more chances.

When Jesus talked about hell, the picture he gave wasn't of a dungeon where bad people are tortured. No—it's much worse. Hell is the place cut off from God's presence and everything good.

Heaven is life with God.

Hell is life without God.

In heaven, God is everywhere.

In hell, God is nowhere.

God contains heaven and you will not be able to avoid him.

HEAVEN IS LIFE WITH GOD. HELL IS LIFE WITHOUT GOD.

In hell, God is absent, and you will not be able to find him.

Isaiah 55:6 reminds us there is a deadline that comes for everyone: "Seek the LORD while he may be found; call on him while he is near."

Hell is the complete absence of God and all the good things that emanate from him. In this world, though life with God is hindered by the presence of sin, we still get to experience some of God, even if we don't want to. God created the world, and it's drenched in tokens of his goodness, such as these:

- Love of family
- Laughter with friends
- Awe of a sunset
- The coo of a baby
- The embrace of a loved one
- Vibrant colors of flowers and fruit
- Beauty of art that moves our souls
- The scent of freshly baked chocolate chip cookies
- Satisfaction received from a job well done
- Pleasure felt in an intimate relationship
- The feeling of hope as the sun rises for a new day

In this life we all experience some of God's presence and goodness. But hell is the place where God and his goodness are not. The land of no more.

In the same way God's presence is what makes heaven, heaven, God's absence is what makes hell, hell.

Hell is life without God and, honestly, what could possibly be worse?

Why Hell?

All of this may raise some disheartening doubts: Why would God allow there to be a hell?

Eternal Life without God

We are eternal creatures, so after this life we need someplace to live out our eternities. God's hope is that all his children will choose to be with him in heaven. But for those who reject him, God honors their free will to choose hell as the place where they can live without him.

But if we're being honest, there are other reasons. These reasons may make us uncomfortable, but I believe they make sense when we examine them with an open mind.

Hell Exists for God to Righteously Punish Satan

God will punish the devil for eternity.

That makes sense when we stop thinking of the devil as a cartoon character in a red suit who whispers in your ear that you should eat the big piece of chocolate cake.

Satan is the embodiment of evil. Behind every addiction, every abuse, behind fear and shame and pain, there is Satan. In the Scriptures he is called the following:

- serpent (Gen. 3:1–19; 2 Cor. 11:3)
- tempter (Matt. 4:3; 1 Thess. 3:5)
- prince of demons (Matt. 12:24)
- father of lies (John 8:44)
- thief (John 10:10)
- roaring lion (1 Peter 5:8)
- evil one (1 John 5:18)
- accuser (Rev. 12:10)

His mission is to steal, kill, and destroy. He wants to steal your health, kill your joy, and destroy your faith. His intention is to ruin your finances, obliterate your marriage, and lead your kids astray.

That's who Satan is, and hell is the place where he will experience the righteous consequences for all his evil. Pastor and author David Platt says, "Hell is not a place where the devil torments sinners; hell is a place where he is tormented *alongside* sinners."[5] We read in Revelation 20:10 that the devil will be thrown into the place where he will be tormented forever.

That sounds fair. Right?

But the next reason for hell we may find even more confusing.

Hell Exists for God to Righteously Punish Evil

This is confusing because none of us thinks we're evil.

As we talked about earlier, we all think we're pretty good.

Some of us admit we sin, and we know sin is bad, but our sin isn't *that* bad. Right? Doesn't God kind of look the other way? He gives us a little wink because it's not that big of a deal? I mean, we're not hurting anyone. Right?

Wrong.

If God ignored our sin, he would not be love. Because sin is toxic and self-destructive, and it damages other people and separates us from God, he wants to protect us from anything that might harm us. Can you imagine a doctor ignoring a lab result that came back showing that her patient had cancer? No, you can't. Because you wouldn't think someone who would do that should be a doctor.

If God ignored our sin, he would not be holy. Because sin is evil and God is just. Can you imagine a judge ignoring a heinous crime presented to him in his courtroom? No, you can't. Because you wouldn't think someone who would do that should be a judge.

That's why we have to remember that it is impossible for God to be holy without being just. As we grow in our understanding of God's character, we'll learn that evil must be punished and that our sin is evil. God's punishment for sin doesn't mean God's not fair; it's actually evidence that God is just.

In 2 Thessalonians 1:9 we read, "They will be punished with everlasting destruction and shut out from the presence of the Lord."

Did you notice that what makes hell, hell is that God is not there? They will be "shut out from the presence of the Lord." Hell is the absence of God and his goodness.

Is that how people in hell will be punished? By being shut out from God and his goodness, or is there more that will happen to them there? I'm not sure, but I don't think there will be anything more excruciatingly torturous than being completely shut out from the presence of God forever.

A Voice from Hell

Jesus told a story about hell in Luke 16 that begins like this: "There was a rich man who was dressed in purple and fine linen and lived in luxury every day" (v. 19). Wearing purple was typically reserved for royalty because the dye was so expensive. In that day, a nice piece of linen could cost as much as a typical person's food for a year.

Sitting at the gate of this rich guy's property was a poor beggar named Lazarus. He was so hungry he longed for the crumbs the stray dogs ate. The same dogs that would lick his sores.

Lazarus died, and angels carried him to Abraham's side. The rich man also died and was taken to Hades, which was known as the place of punishment for the dead.

Jesus' story shows how the tables on earth can take a dramatic turn in eternity. Rich Dude was in agony in Hades when he looked up and saw Abraham far away with Lazarus by his side. He called out, "Father Abraham, have pity on me and send Lazarus to dip the tip of his finger in water and cool my tongue, because I am in agony in this fire" (v. 24). Tortured, he wanted a little relief from his suffering.

Abraham told him no one could travel between the two places, so Rich Dude made a different request. "Then I beg you, father, send Lazarus to my family, for I have five brothers. Let him warn them, so that they will not also come to this place of torment" (vv. 27–28).

Here are four things we learn about hell from Jesus' story:

1. **THE RICH MAN WAS FULLY CONSCIOUS AND AWARE.** He had his memory. He was in pain. He was full of regrets.
2. **THE RICH MAN'S ETERNITY WAS IRREVOCABLE.** It was too late to change his fate from the land of no more chances.
3. **THE RICH MAN KNEW HIS SUFFERING WAS JUST.** How do we know that? He complained about the *pain* but never about the *punishment*. He said it was horrible but not that it was unfair.

4. **THE RICH MAN PLEADED FOR SOMEONE TO TELL HIS BROTHERS THAT THEIR CHOICES HAD AN ETERNAL IMPACT.** He knew his brothers would end up where he was unless they made a different choice, so he begged for someone to warn them.

To me, that last one is the most powerful aspect of the story. This man, as self-consumed as he may have been, loved his brothers. When you love someone, you desperately don't want them to go to hell.

That's why we must talk about the subject that no one wants to talk about.

And that's why God sent Jesus.

A Way Out

Hell exists because we are eternal creatures. We need a place to go forever after we die.

God gave you the free will to choose life with him or without him. God sent his Son, Jesus, so you would know how much he loves you and that, no matter what you've done, he is still inviting you to be with him.

Hell exists because there needs to be a place for God to righteously punish evil, and our sin is evil. We have all sinned. Romans 3:23 says that "all have sinned and fall short of the glory of God."

While the Bible is clear about "all," you may be thinking, *But I'm a good person. I have a good heart.* Actually, we have deceitful hearts, and we are all sinful people. We have lied, stolen, and deceived. We have worshiped idols—we just don't think of it as worship and don't call them idols. Even when we do good things, some of them are tainted by impure motives.

Admittedly, sin is a very unpopular subject in today's culture. But just because it's unpopular doesn't mean it's untrue. It's imperative that we acknowledge our sinfulness. Why? Because if we don't see ourselves as sinners, we won't see our need for a Savior.

We are not good. God is good. We are not holy. God is holy. Because he is holy, he must be just. Because he is just, he must punish sin.

God is good, holy, and just—and he is love. Love isn't just what he does. Love is who he is. Because he is love, God sent Jesus. "But God demonstrates his own love for us in this: While we were still sinners, Christ died for us" (Rom. 5:8).

His death and resurrection make all the difference. Romans 3 says we all sin, but also that "all are justified freely by his grace through the redemption that came by Christ Jesus. God presented Christ as a sacrifice of atonement, through the shedding of his blood—to be received by faith" (Rom. 3:24–25).

Based on these verses, if we choose Jesus by faith, he does the following:

- Justifies us as if we've never sinned
- Freely gives grace to us, which is the opposite of what we deserve
- Redeems us and saves us
- Makes atonement for us and removes our sin

How good is that? No matter how gross your sin, God's grace is greater. By grace, through faith, God covers all your sins.

- Your jealousy: forgiven.
- Your lust: forgotten.
- Your lies: pardoned.
- Your deception: blotted out.
- Your pride: erased.
- Your cheating: wiped away.
- Your guilt: cleansed.

When you confess your sins and hand everything over to him, he is faithful and just and will forgive and purify you (1 John 1:9). Jesus offers grace, not guilt or grief. There is now no condemnation for those who, through their faith, are in Christ (Rom. 8:1).

Why Would God Send Someone to Hell?

So the big question with which so many people wrestle is this: Why would God send someone to hell?

I hope the answer is clear by now.

He doesn't.

GOD DOESN'T SEND PEOPLE TO HELL. PEOPLE CHOOSE HELL.

God doesn't send people to hell. People choose hell.

They choose hell when they reject life with God and choose to do life on their own as their own god. Hell is simply the result of that choice.

They choose hell whenever they ignore or deny their sin. Hell is the necessary consequence of those choices.

They choose hell when they say no to Jesus and what he did on the cross for them. Hell is where we pay for our sins if we don't let Jesus pay for them.

In their argument about heaven and hell, some people say, "Everyone wants into the eternal pleasure factory of heaven, but God is trying to keep people out, which is mean and exclusive." No. The reality is that many people don't want life with God in heaven, but even still, God is trying to bring everyone in. And, in Jesus, he provided a way for everyone to get in.

God doesn't want anyone to go to hell; that's why he sent Jesus for everyone. "The Lord is not slow in keeping his promise, as some understand slowness. Instead he is patient with you, not wanting anyone to perish, but everyone to come to repentance" (2 Peter 3:9).

God is patient with you. He's waiting for you. He's working on you. He's reaching out to you. He's sending people your way. He has sent this book your way. He's drawing you to himself by his Spirit. Because he is love, God doesn't want anyone to perish but wants "everyone to come to repentance."

The same is true for those you love who don't know Jesus. He's patient. He's waiting. He's drawing them by his Spirit. He wants them free from the pain of sin and to experience his goodness on earth and for eternity.

That's why God doesn't send us to hell. He sent Jesus to save us from hell.

The devil comes to steal, kill, and destroy.

Jesus comes that you might have life and life more abundantly.

We don't have to go to hell, because Jesus came to give us eternal life with God, and that life starts now.

Eternal Life, Starting Now

Take a moment to think about that person you know who has a long history of making really bad choices. Life seems to always be a mess and getting worse. Now think about a Christian you know who is walking with Jesus every day and is an example to you.

Comparing those two lives, isn't it fair to say that we can see how eternal life begins in the here and now? The effects of both heaven and hell are very real and visible starting here on earth. While God has made every life to be eternal, there is a huge difference when Jesus brings us into *his* eternal life. And, thank God, even that person you thought of first, as long as he or she is still breathing, can surrender to Jesus and change everything. But enough about other people.

Jesus came to give *you* eternal life.

Some assume eternal life is just about quantity—meaning looooong life—life forever.

But that's not all. God created us to be eternal creatures and we are going to live looooong forever lives, with or without Jesus.

Jesus said, "Now this is eternal life: that they know you, the only true God, and Jesus Christ, whom you have sent" (John 17:3). He didn't say eternal life is never-ending life. He said eternal life is knowing the one true God and his Son, Jesus.

Eternal life is about quality, not just quantity. Eternal life is the abundant life Jesus offers, which we will experience fully in heaven, but that life begins now.

When you start living life with God, there are positive consequences that Galatians 5:22–23 calls fruit: love, joy, peace, patience, kindness, goodness, faithfulness, gentleness, and self-control, which come with the presence of a good God. He will comfort you, guide you, open doors for you, provide for you, give you strength when you're weak and peace when you're afraid. Of course, life won't be perfect until we get to heaven, but it starts getting better *now*.

In the same way that hell is the place of no more good things, heaven is the place of no more bad things. In Revelation 21:3, John heard a loud voice from heaven that said, "Look! God's dwelling place is now among the people, and he will dwell with them. They will be his people, and God himself will be with them and be their God." There it is again: "God will dwell with them." Why? Because God loves us. God's greatest desire is to show us his love.

> **IN THE SAME WAY THAT HELL IS THE PLACE OF NO MORE GOOD THINGS, HEAVEN IS THE PLACE OF NO MORE BAD THINGS.**

Heaven is the presence of God.

In the presence of God, Revelation 21 tells us that "'he will wipe every tear from their eyes. There will be no more death' or mourning or crying or pain, for the old order of things has passed away" (v. 4).

Imagine that. Heaven is also the land of no more. In God's presence you will experience this:

- No more headaches.
- No more depression.
- No more rejection.
- No more bullying.
- No more financial pressure.
- No more loneliness.
- No more fear.
- No more insecurities.
- No more temptation.

- No more guilt.
- No more shame.
- No more death.
- No more mourning.
- No more crying.
- No more pain.

God loves you more than you will ever know. He wants you to be with him forever. And God wants you to have peace about what will happen to you after you die, because you've put your faith in Jesus. And because your faith is in Jesus, even if you fall back into some old sin, his grace will cover you because there is no condemnation for those who are in Christ.

That's why I want everyone to know him. Because I didn't for so long. I only knew *about* him.

I tried to be good enough for him. But that didn't work. It seemed as though the harder I tried, the worse I got. I could never be good enough.

That's why I want everyone to know how good he is. That's why I want *you* to know how good he is. Even though we've done wrong and been sinful, he loves us just as we are.

So much that he sent Jesus for us.

Jesus came to keep you out of hell, but, more than that, Jesus came to give you eternal life.

And that life starts now.

> Since you have been raised to new life with Christ, set your sights on the realities of heaven, where Christ sits in the place of honor at God's right hand. Think about the things of heaven, not the things of earth.
>
> —Colossians 3:1–2 NLT

CHAPTER 8 EXERCISES

1. Do you tend to avoid thinking or talking about hell? Explain.

2. Why do you suppose most people want to avoid the subject of hell?

3. Why do you think there are so many different wrong ideas about both heaven and hell?

4. As Christians, why is it important for us to understand the biblical realities of both heaven and hell?

5. What are your thoughts on John Ortberg's statement: "Heaven does not contain God; God contains heaven"?

6. What are your thoughts on these statements: "Heaven is life with God. Hell is life without God" and "In heaven, God is everywhere. In hell, God is nowhere"?

7. In reading the sections about hell existing for God to righteously punish Satan and evil, did you gain any new insight or understanding? Explain.

8. In your opinion, what is the most important takeaway about hell from Jesus' story of the rich man and Lazarus in Luke 16?

9. Do you agree with the statement "God doesn't send people to hell. People choose hell"? Why or why not?

10. How do you feel about the idea that eternal life can start today and continue into eternity?

CHAPTER 9

Why Believe the Bible If Science Contradicts It?

I was a college freshman taking a BibLit class. You might be wondering whether "BibLit" means "That bib is really lit." Nope. BibLit is short for biblical literature.

As I mentioned previously, I was not following Christ in college. But since I attended a small liberal arts Christian school, everyone was required to take BibLit. The class was at 8:00 in the morning, and if I wasn't hungover, it was only because I was still drunk.

One day, my professor talked about some verse in the Old Testament. (Which verse? I don't remember. Like I said, I was not in the best head-space.) He explained that what the Bible said in this verse could not possibly be true. (Ironic that I experienced this not only at a Christian college but also, as I told you in chapter 1, at seminary.) As I listened, my very limited, very undeveloped faith crumbled. I had been pretty certain I believed in God with a basic cultural assumption that what the Bible said was true. But here was an educated professor using science to contradict Scripture, and my feeble faith quickly fell apart.

Have you ever been there?

Perhaps you've always believed God created the world in seven days, but someone confronted you with what science says about the age of the earth and evolution. Maybe you believed that God created life out of his love, but then a teacher said we evolved in a random occurrence called the "primordial soup theory." Or that your original ancestor was not a man in a garden but an ape in a tree. And when those people sounded far more confident in science than you felt in your faith, that opened a big door to doubt.

You started to question whether the Bible and science are in conflict with each other, eventually asking yourself, *Can I be an intelligent, educated person and still believe all the Christian stuff I'm supposed to believe?*

This conflict between science and faith reminds me of the fifth-grade girl who shared the Bible story of Jonah with her class. Her teacher immediately told her it was impossible for a whale to swallow Jonah and for him to live in its stomach. Because the little girl had learned the story in Sunday school, she stood her ground, insisting, "I know it happened because it's in the Bible." The teacher retorted, "No, it's impossible." The little girl said, "Yes, it happened." The teacher maintained, "No, it didn't." The girl started crying and said, "Then when I get to heaven, I'll ask Jonah, and he'll tell me it *did* happen." The teacher wouldn't back down. She asked, "Well, what if Jonah's in hell?" The little girl told her, "Well, then when you die, *you* ask him!"

Like this fifth grader, the challenge to our faith can start early. So many people decide to follow Jesus and believe what the Bible says, but then

- they read an article from some "reputable source" that contradicts what they think about God.
- they watch a video on YouTube that "proves" the Bible wrong.
- a friend points out a supposed flaw in what they believe.
- a ton of people pile on arguing against a spiritual post they put on their Instagram.
- a professor belittles their faith using "evidence" from science.

Before long, their faith starts to falter.
Can you relate?

Have you ever felt as if you had to make a choice and take a side?

You start to assume science and the Bible are in conflict and doubt whether you can believe in both.

But what if that assumption is wrong?

What if science and the Bible are not competitive but cooperative?

What if science and the Bible can actually work together to help us grow closer to God?

The Battle That Doesn't Exist

The God of science is also the God of the Bible. He's given us both, and each is meant to reveal him to us.

For instance, Psalm 19 starts out like this:

> The heavens proclaim the glory of God.
> The skies display his craftsmanship.
> Day after day they continue to speak;
>   night after night they make him known.
> They speak without a sound or word;
>   their voice is never heard.
> Yet their message has gone throughout the earth,
>   and their words to all the world.
>
> —PSALM 19:1–4 NLT

> **THE GOD OF SCIENCE IS ALSO THE GOD OF THE BIBLE, AND EACH IS MEANT TO REVEAL HIM TO US.**

The psalmist David is saying that nature (the realm of science) reveals God. He continues:

> The instructions of the LORD are perfect,
>   reviving the soul.
> The decrees of the LORD are trustworthy,
>   making wise the simple.
> The commandments of the LORD are right,
>   bringing joy to the heart.

> The commands of the LORD are clear,
>> giving insight for living. . . .
> The laws of the LORD are true;
>> each one is fair.
> They are more desirable than gold,
>> even the finest gold.
> They are sweeter than honey,
>> even honey dripping from the comb.
>
> —PSALM 19:7–10 NLT

David is saying God's Word gives us life and wisdom and joy.

God has revealed himself through nature *and* Scripture. You might say that he's given us two books: the "book" of God's *world* and the book of God's *Word*—written by the same sovereign author—that go together hand in hand.

Paul made this connection in Romans 1:20: "For ever since the world was created, people have seen the earth and sky. Through everything God made, they can clearly see his invisible qualities—his eternal power and divine nature. So they have no excuse for not knowing God" (NLT).

About four hundred years after the birth of Christ, a brilliant theologian and philosopher named Augustine understood that science and the Bible are complementary, not competitive. He taught that the faith-versus-science conflict comes from either misunderstanding science or misinterpreting the Bible.

For instance, let's take a look at perhaps the most famous example of the supposed conflict between science and the Bible. In the 1600s, both the church and scientific community believed the sun revolved around the earth.

Why would they think that? Good question.

It just seemed right to them. And to validate that scientific belief with Scripture they would point to Psalm 104:5: "You placed the world on its foundation so it would never be moved" (NLT).

Then an Italian physicist and astronomer named Galileo made a discovery. Using more powerful telescopes than had been available in the past, he discovered the "stellar parallax"—basically that the night sky would not look the way it did if the earth was the center of the universe. He wrote *Dialogue Concerning the Two Chief World Systems*, proposing that a conversation start between theologians and scientists.

But the church said no. They asserted that the Earth was the center of the universe, tried Galileo for heresy, and, finding him guilty, put him under house arrest for the rest of his life.

Is that an example of the incompatibility between science and the Bible?

No.

The supposed contradiction came because of a misinterpretation of the Bible. "You placed the world on its foundation so it would never be moved" did not mean the earth was the center of the universe. That's obvious to us now and should have been obvious to them, but people back then had a flawed interpretation. (Interestingly, that misinterpretation of the Bible was originally based on scientists' misunderstanding of the world.)

God is the God of science and the God of Scripture, and a belief that they are in conflict comes from misunderstanding one or the other.

The truth is not found in science *or* the Bible.

The truth is found in science *and* the Bible.

These two ideas lead me to some important *what if* questions:

- What if the relationship between science and the Bible isn't meant to be competitive?
- What if it's meant to be cooperative?
- What if it's meant to be complementary?
- What if, instead of either/or, it's both/and?

> THE TRUTH IS NOT FOUND IN SCIENCE *OR* THE BIBLE. THE TRUTH IS FOUND IN SCIENCE *AND* THE BIBLE.

We love both/and, don't we?

If your kid has a birthday, you don't say, "We can have chocolate cake *or* vanilla ice cream." There is no *or*. It's both/and.

You don't have a peanut butter *or* a jelly sandwich. There is no *or*, it's both/and.

Do you ask someone to put the salt *or* pepper shaker on the table? No. Both/and.

Eggs or bacon? Both/and. (Actually, both/and/and—eggs and bacon, and more bacon.)

Batman and Robin.

Netflix and chill. (But only if you're married!)

We like both/and, and Christians should embrace both/and more than others because both/and is a prominent feature of our faith.

- Jesus said, "I am the Alpha *and* the Omega, the First *and* the Last, the Beginning *and* the End" (Rev. 22:13).
- Jesus "came from the Father, full of grace *and* truth" (John 1:14).
- Jesus is the "author *and* finisher of our faith" (Heb. 12:2 NKJV).

Then there's the "eggs and bacon, and more bacon" verse, John 14:6: "I am the way and the truth and the life."

So I would suggest to you: God is the God of science *and* the Bible.

Two Tools with Two Purposes

In your garage or miscellaneous drawer you probably have some tools. Each of those tools has a purpose. You can attempt to use a tool for the wrong purpose, but it won't go well. Try hammering with a wrench and you may do more damage to the wrench than the nail. Sawing with a screwdriver? Totally ineffective. Scissors to cut wood? Good luck. Different tools have different purposes.

If you see a guy at the beach with a metal detector, you know what he's doing because of the tool he's using. He's looking for—what *is* he looking for? Diamond rings? Quarters? I've never been sure. But one thing I do know: he's not trying to find sand. Metal detectors detect metal, not sand. You know a metal detector has one distinct purpose.

When you look inside a toolbox, you know two things: First, everything in there is the same—they're all tools. Second, each tool is different and has its own purpose.

One reason some have the impression that the Bible and science are at odds, or that science has disproven the Bible, is because they don't have clarity on what each is really about.

In one sense they are similar because, at their core, each presents truth. Yet this can lead to confusion when each, in presenting truth, also offers different answers.

Why is that?

Because they're not centered on the same kind of truth.

Science is based on what we can observe. Remember the scientific method in school? You

- make an observation,
- form a question,
- come up with a hypothesis,
- conduct an experiment,
- analyze the data, and
- draw a conclusion.

> SCIENCE IS DEFINED BY THAT WHICH CAN BE OBSERVED. FAITH IS BASED ON WHAT *CANNOT* BE OBSERVED.

Science is defined by, and limited to, that which can be observed.

Faith is based on what *cannot* be observed. The truth of the Bible has to be taken in faith. We're told in Hebrews 11:1, "Now faith is confidence in what we hope for and assurance about what we do not see." Later in that same chapter we are told that one of the fathers of our faith, Moses, "persevered because he saw him who is invisible" (v. 27). The Bible says of Christians, "For we live by faith, not by sight" (2 Cor. 5:7).

Faith is about believing in and living for something that is *not* observable, measurable, or repeatable. First Thessalonians 2:13 tells us, "When you received his message from us, you didn't think of our words as mere human ideas. You accepted what we said as the very word of God—which, of course, it is. And this word continues to work in you who believe" (NLT).

Science and Scripture both offer truth, but different kinds of truth, which can give the impression they're at odds, but they're not. Each is concerned with different truths and employs different methods of allowing people to discover those truths. Therefore, they won't always come to the same conclusions.

This also means the different answers they find are not mutually exclusive. Like that guy using the metal detector—those are great at finding metal, but they detect metal under the sand. They do not detect sand. Of course, that does not mean the sand doesn't exist. It also doesn't mean the palm trees on the beach or the ocean lapping up against it doesn't exist. Metal detectors simply aren't designed to detect that which is not metal. In the same way, science is a very effective tool in studying the natural world, but that does not mean the *super*natural world that the Bible teaches does not exist.

Science seeks truth about our natural world. Scripture is a different tool that reveals truth about the supernatural world. Science and Scripture can and do work together. Why? Because they point us to the same God.

Clarity or Faith?

One of the reasons we think science and Scripture contradict each other is because we're confused about the goals of each.

The goal of science is to produce clarity.

The goal of the Bible is to produce faith.

John Kavanaugh was a professor of philosophy at Saint Louis University. He spent a year searching for purpose in life and then moved to Calcutta, India, to help Mother Teresa in her ministry of serving the poor. One day she asked Kavanaugh, "What can I pray for you?" He thought, *This is it. My moment!* So he asked Mother Teresa to please pray for clarity. She said no, telling him, "Clarity is the last thing you are clinging to and must let go of." He was taken aback and sputtered out, "But you seem to have clarity. Why won't you pray for me to have clarity?" Mother

Teresa stated, "I've never had clarity, what I've always had is trust. That's what I will pray for you. That you will trust God."[1]

Perhaps you've been asking questions your whole life, looking for clarity, wanting to find an unquestionably clear and understood grasp on life. That's not bad. It's good. Keep looking. But at some point you may realize what you need more than clarity is faith.

And I would encourage you to not view Christianity as being about having all the right answers. It's not. Christianity is about a faith in Jesus that gives you a vital relationship with God, the one who does hold all the answers.

Needing absolute clarity and having every right answer is taking a scientific, not faith-filled, approach. If you feel you have to have every right answer, you may be building your faith on a house of cards instead of on the person of Jesus Christ. Then, when one of your beliefs about God is challenged, your entire faith system can crumble. That's what happened to hungover me in my 8:00 a.m. BibLit class. My fragile faith couldn't handle one simple challenge. I was ready to give up on God.

That's crazy. We shouldn't give up when one piece of our faith gets challenged. But so many do.

There is one way we may want to take a more scientific approach to our faith. Remember, with the scientific method you start with a hypothesis, then you run an experiment to test it, which produces results, which leads you to a conclusion. If your hypothesis is disproven, do you give up on science?

No. You realize you have to come up with a different hypothesis, so you ask more questions and pursue a deeper understanding. Then you come up with a new hypothesis and do another test to determine whether you got it right this time.

Why don't we take that approach as Christians about our faith?

If we realize there's a challenge to our beliefs about God, we don't give up on God. We view it as an opportunity to grow our faith. So we ask more questions. We pursue a deeper understanding of what the Bible says or who God really is.

We don't walk away from God just because something wasn't exactly the way we thought. We realize that God and his Word are infallible but that our understanding *is* fallible. We apply the scientific approach to our faith.

Have you noticed our understanding often changes over time? Scientists once believed the earth was flat and that bloodletting through leeches was the best way to cure illness and that doctors didn't need to wash their hands. Christians used to believe playing cards and dancing and going to movies were sinful. Everyone used to think the four original flavors of Pop-Tarts were enough. (They were strawberry, blueberry, brown sugar, and apple currant.) (Apple *currant*? What is a currant?)

> IF THERE'S A CHALLENGE TO OUR BELIEFS ABOUT GOD, DON'T GIVE UP BUT VIEW IT AS AN OPPORTUNITY TO GROW OUR FAITH.

My point? You are never going to have perfect clarity or get all the answers exactly right. If that's what you need, it will eventually create problems, as well as doubts. As Mother Teresa told John Kavanaugh, what you really need is faith, a growing trust in Jesus.

Merging Science and Scripture

Let's look at two interactions between science and Scripture that are examples of issues causing some to question their faith. I believe these can actually build our faith.

The Beginning of Everything

One of the best places to see science and Scripture work together is in the very first verse of the Bible, Genesis 1:1: "In the beginning God created the heavens and the earth." More than three thousand years ago, Scripture declared what science finally confirmed in the last one hundred years: the universe had a beginning.

Prior to the big bang theory, most atheist scientists claimed the universe was eternal. In the 1700s, philosopher Immanuel Kant popularized this view, saying the universe had no beginning and would have no end.[2] Christians, of course, believed the universe began at a specific moment, when God brought it into existence.

In 1905, Albert Einstein discovered the theory of relativity, which claimed there were additional laws governing the universe. Then, in 1915, Einstein announced that equations based on the theory of relativity revealed the universe was not infinite, that it was expanding and had to have begun at a certain point in time.[3]

Scientists fought against Einstein. Why?

I think believing the universe is eternal was convenient for many of them. If the universe had a beginning, it would only make sense that it had a begin*ner*. You would almost have to believe there was a catalyst outside of the universe that brought it into existence.

His fellow scientists' argument against Einstein was that if everything began with an explosion, there would be leftover radiation throughout the universe. Since there was no such radiation, the universe had always existed and did not need a creator.

Until 1992.

That was the year scientists discovered the previously undetectable radiation in the background of our cosmos. They now knew without a doubt that the universe had a beginning. George Smoot, the University of California at Berkeley astronomer and leading scientist on the project that discovered the radiation, said, "What we have found is evidence for the birth of the universe. . . . It's like looking at God."[4]

Science and Scripture had always seemed to contradict each other, but, in this case, science caught up with Scripture and confirmed what the Bible had always said. What had seemed like a conflict had actually been a misunderstanding.

Not competing but complementary and cooperative.

The Design of the Universe

Earlier, I gave you the first verse in the Bible. The next place to see science and Scripture work together is in the second verse, Genesis 1:2: "Now the earth was formless and empty, darkness was over the surface of the deep, and the Spirit of God was hovering over the waters." Then God watched Chip and Joanna Gaines on *Fixer Upper* and decided it was time to start organizing everything. He designed everything in the most beautiful way, so it all worked together perfectly.

It's mind-blowing when you think about it. Someone puts a seed in the ground. God sends rain from heaven. The rain falls onto the ground and the water seeps down into the soil. The seed takes root and, before long, pushes through the dirt as it sprouts up and grows into a plant. Then, one day, with more rain and the right amount of sun, it buds and there's fruit. An animal eats the fruit and people eat the animal. (Unless they've watched that Netflix show on why we shouldn't eat meat.) Eventually the animals and people die and go into the ground and fertilize the soil and the whole process continues. (My kids and I first learned this from Mufasa's "circle of life" lesson to Simba.)

Scientists today affirm what Christians have believed for a long time. They have established what is known as the "anthropic principle"—the universe appears to be designed for human life. More than a century of astronomy and physics research reveals that the emergence of humans and civilization requires physical constants, laws, and properties that fall within certain narrow ranges. This truth applies also to the galaxy and planetary system. This principle of physical evidence points to humanity as the central theme of the cosmos. By the end of 2001, astronomers had identified about 150 different constants that are perfectly designed to support intelligent physical life on earth.[5]

- If the Earth were tilted on its axis just a bit more or less, we'd all die.
- If the Earth spun a little faster or slower, we'd all die.
- If the average distance from the Earth to the sun were three-tenths of 1 percent closer or farther, we'd all die.

All of this is why an atheist scientist, Roger Penrose, calculated the likelihood of the universe "accidentally" having this precise of a design needed for human life to exist on Earth at 1 in $10^{10^{123}}$.[6] That's one in ten billion—with an extra 123 zeros after you put all the zeros needed to represent ten billion. Those are impossible odds. You would have a better chance of winning the lottery ten thousand times in a row and getting struck by lightning every time you go to cash in your winning ticket.

The psalmist wrote, "The heavens declare the glory of God; the skies proclaim the work of his hands" (Ps. 19:1). Today, science helps us to understand how true that is.

I hope you see how science, rather than causing you to question your faith, can actually increase your confidence in your faith.

While there are a few well-known scientists who attack the Christian faith, there are many others who claim the Christian faith.

And, instead of the science of scientists leading faithful people away from their faith, the faith of faithful people can lead scientists *to* faith.

> RATHER THAN CAUSING YOU TO QUESTION YOUR FAITH, SCIENCE CAN ACTUALLY INCREASE YOUR CONFIDENCE IN YOUR FAITH.

(In a quick web search of renowned scientists and Christian faith, you can find amazing quotes from Robert Boyle, Michael Faraday, Isaac Newton, and Carl Gauss, to name a few.)

What Do You Believe?

Francis Collins is a physician-geneticist. He led the Human Genome Project as director of the National Human Genome Research Institute and then was appointed the director of the National Institutes of Health, a role in which he served from 2009 to 2021 under three presidents.

He was raised outside the church and without faith. Incredibly intelligent, he got his PhD in chemistry at Yale, then went on to receive an MD at the University of North Carolina.

As a staunch atheist, Collins believed science gave all the answers any person ever needed. He said he avoided Christians in college because he thought they were weird.

But then something happened.

In his third year of medical school, he started having to sit at the bedside of terminally ill patients facing death. He was perplexed by how so many of them had peace. Collins said, "They talked about their faith, and I thought, *Why aren't you angry at God? Why aren't you shaking your fist at what God has done to you?*"

Collins couldn't understand. "They were at peace. They felt like God had been good to them. They had been blessed, and they looked forward to what came after. I was not going to look forward to what came after, from my perspective. So I was a little troubled by that."

One elderly woman had a cardiac disease that created intense chest pain. There was nothing doctors or medicine could do for her.

Collins watched her during each episode of excruciating chest pain and noticed, "She would pray with the greatest earnestness I'd ever seen. And then she would come through it and would still seem at peace."

Day after day she shared her faith with Collins until, finally, she said, "Doctor, I've shared my faith with you, and you seem to be somebody who cares for me. What do you believe?"

Like a sudden punch to the gut, Collins realized no one had ever asked him that question and that, even more surprising, he had no answer. He stammered out a response, "Well, I don't think I really know." He wrote later, "I realized I'd really neglected the most important question that any of us ever asks: Is there a God, and does that God care about me?"

That moment led him on a journey in which he examined the world's religions and eventually read a book by C. S. Lewis called *Mere Christianity*.

One day while hiking in the beauty of God's creation in the Cascade Mountains, Collins fell to his knees and told Jesus, "I get it. I'm yours. I want to be your follower from now until eternity."[7]

Science had given him answers, but it didn't give him *the* answer.

Science didn't give him a solution to his sin problem.

Science didn't give him something to put his trust in.

Science didn't give him the unconditional, perfect love he longed for.

Finally, he found something—someone—who could do all of that. Jesus.

In Collins' 2006 book *The Language of God: A Scientist Presents Evidence for Belief*, he states:

> Will we turn our backs on science because it is perceived as a threat to God, abandoning all the promise of advancing our understanding of nature and applying that to the alleviation of suffering and the betterment of humankind? Alternatively, will we turn our backs on faith, concluding that science has rendered the spiritual life no longer necessary, and that traditional religious symbols can now be replaced by engravings of the double helix on our altars? Both of these choices are profoundly dangerous. Both deny truth. Both will diminish the nobility of humankind. Both will be devastating to our future. And both are unnecessary. The God of the Bible is also the God of the genome. He can be worshiped in the cathedral or in the laboratory.[8]

Science is good. And science is not in conflict with faith and the Bible.

Science can give you some answers about the natural world, but I'm convinced what you need is a real encounter and a forever relationship with a supernatural God.

Science can't give you that.

Faith can.

"Where were you when I laid the earth's foundation? Tell me, if you understand. Who marked off its dimensions? Surely you know! Who stretched a measuring line across it? On what were its footings set, or who laid its cornerstone—while the morning stars sang together and all the angels shouted for joy?"

—Job 38:4–7

CHAPTER 9 EXERCISE

1. What was your first experience of someone challenging your faith with science? What happened, and how did you respond?

2. Why do you think science and the Bible have often been pitted against each other to compete for truth?

3. What are your thoughts on the statement that God has revealed himself through nature and Scripture—"The book of God's *world* and the book of God's *Word*"?

4. Believing God is the Creator, why would it be important to understand that truth is found in both science and the Bible—both/and?

5. What are your thoughts on science being about what *can* be observed and faith being about what *cannot* be observed?

6. After reading Francis Collins' testimony and the Christian patient's question to him, why do you think the acceptance of the gospel always has to come down to receiving God's love by faith, not through clarification of facts and answers?

7. How do discoveries such as the anthropic principle and testimonies like Francis Collins' help us deepen our faith in the truths of the Bible?

8. How could growing in your knowledge and understanding of the Bible help you navigate all faith challenges, including from the scientific community?

9. What is your response to Collins' quote "The God of the Bible is also the God of the genome. He can be worshiped in the cathedral or in the laboratory"?

10. What was your main takeaway from this chapter?

CHAPTER 10

Why Would God Love Me?

When I put my faith in Jesus, I left the bar scene.

Now, just a few months later, I was back.

Why?

Drunk people like to talk about God.

That's why I was in the bar.

No, really.

I wanted to share how Jesus had changed my life with the guys who were still where I was not that long ago. I wanted them to hear about what I had found.

One particular night, I was sharing about God's love with this guy whose slobbering words needed a little deciphering. As best as I could discern, he was saying, "I loz you. I wazzed to tellzz you, I weally luuv you, man!"

I smiled. "Thank you."

"Wasss youz name again?" he asked.

"Craig."

"So Greg—"

"No, Craig."

"Craig." He looked me right in the eye. "I love you. Like, willy. I mean weally. I love you, like, a lot."

I shared, again, that God loved him. He was doubtful but interested. In fact, he said, "The music ezzz tooooo loud. Cans weez go outside so I'z can hear you b-better?" As soon as we walked out of the bar, I immediately heard a voice, an amplified voice. Across the street, there was a flatbed trailer with a street preacher up on his portable platform.

My first thought was "Oh, thank God! Reinforcements! I worked on the guy inside. This guy's got him outside. We're gonna tag team him!"

What I didn't realize is that this guy was one of those angry street preachers. He pointed right at me, not my drunk friend, and yelled, "You're going to hell, you fornicatin' sinner!"

I was like, "Dude, no. I mean, I *was* a fornicatin' sinner going to hell. But not anymore! Now I'm going to heaven. But this guy *is* going to hell. That's why I'm here, working on Drunk Buddy."

Angry Street Preacher was not convinced. He kept pointing at me and got even louder. "No! You're going to hell unless you turn from your sins and repent!"

Drunk Buddy—who, did I mention, loved me a lot—looked at me, then looked back at the guy, and said, "No. No! I says no! Heeez not going to hell." Then he pointed at Angry Street Preacher and announced, "You is the one who is gonna be goin' to hell. Cuz I's about to send you there!"

Drunk Buddy started rushing toward Angry Street Preacher's make-shift stage! He somehow managed to run at him, and I took chase. Fortunately, he wasn't exactly going in a straight line, so I caught up pretty quick, grabbed him, and tried to calm him down. "Dude, you can't just go around beating people up."

What he said next surprised me. Drunk Buddy went from really loving to really angry to really sad, and whimpered, "See! I knew God doesn't love me. I told you . . . waz your name again?"

"Craig."

"Yes! You're right! I told you, Greg."

"It's Craig."

"Right. I told you God doesn't love me, like ever, at all." Drunk Buddy started crying. "I done too many things wrong. He could never love me."

"No," I insisted, "God does love you."

"No, Craig, I'm nothing. Coz of too much sin. Thaz all I am, a sinner."

The louder he cried, the more I tried to convince him. "No, dude, you need to understand. God does love you."

"No, Craig, he doesn't. He doesn't love me."

Even though I knew Drunk Buddy's thought of "God doesn't love me" was biblically and theologically wrong, I also understood how it was easy for him to believe.

Full disclosure: when I have told this story before, I've left out one detail. Like my inebriated pal, I, too, have struggled to believe God loves me.

I've now been a pastor for more than thirty years, and when people open up to me, I find this to be one of the most common and heart-wrenching doubts. So many people are convinced *God may love everyone else, but there's no way he loves . . . me.* Somehow, many of us seem to have bought into the lie that all the many "God loves us" verses in the Bible have one lone exception.

When I ask questions and try to dig into that doubt, I typically find two distorted beliefs:

1. I'm too insignificant.
2. I'm too sinful.

But I'm Too Insignificant

The common question is "Who am I to be loved by God?"

Aaron was about thirty years old and trying to recover from a painful divorce that, by his own admission, was mostly his fault. After five years of marriage and two daughters, Aaron told me he got bored. So instead of seeking a fun activity to enjoy with his wife or taking up a new hobby, Aaron fell back into his old habit of watching porn. At first he just looked, but, as often happens, soon that was not enough, which led to acting out. Fighting back tears, Aaron told me about his many sexual sins. After his wife caught him the first time, she was devastated but worked to forgive

Aaron and salvage their marriage for the sake of their daughters. When she caught him a second time, she filed for divorce. "With all I've done," Aaron mumbled almost to himself, "who am I to be loved by God?"

That's a feeling that can easily become a doubt lurking in the shadows of our minds. But the problem is that doubts rarely stay doubts. They can eventually become toxic beliefs. Beliefs that get harder and harder for faith to overcome.

If you can relate to Aaron's feelings, I've got good news. If you're not sure whether God could love you, you're thinking of the wrong kind of love.

It's important that we understand there are two types of love.

> IF YOU'RE NOT SURE WHETHER GOD COULD LOVE YOU, YOU'RE THINKING OF THE WRONG KIND OF LOVE.

THE FIRST IS A LOVE THAT LOVES BECAUSE THE OBJECT IS VALUABLE. This is the love we see most often, when one is drawn to an object because it's viewed as expensive or important or attractive. It's why teenage girls love Tom Holland, and your neighbor loves her new marble countertops, and the guy at work loves his midlife-crisis sports car. It's why, growing up, you loved your Barbie doll or baseball card collection. The first love—one we see all the time—loves because the object is valuable to the person.

This is the kind of love that has led so many of us to feel invaluable and unlovable. Perhaps you weren't quite attractive, athletic, talented, or smart enough. That was disappointing, but what was disheartening was the response of others. You were never as popular as you wanted to be. Your family seemed to be perpetually let down. Because of that, you couldn't even imagine how far short you fell from God's expectations. You became resigned to the idea that no one could ever really love you because you're just not valuable enough.

Fortunately, there's a second type of love.

THE SECOND LOVE GIVES VALUE TO THE OBJECT BEING LOVED. This love doesn't love because the object is valuable. Instead, it bestows value.

I'll show you what I mean.

Think back for a moment and remember your favorite childhood cuddle toy. You might have had a teddy bear, or a stuffed monkey, or a blankie. Whatever it was, it probably didn't cost much to begin with, and I bet it became very flawed. You dragged it around so much that it may have been torn or gotten a hole in it. Your cuddle toy may have started to smell gross because you held it close and sweated all over it on hot summer nights. You may have played with it out in your yard and gotten it really dirty. Even though your toy was flawed, you loved it anyway.

My cuddle toy was Bobby the Bear.

To be clear, there was nothing valuable about my bear. He wasn't expensive. He wasn't a collector's item. He didn't talk or play music.

But I loved Bobby the Bear.

All right, I'm going to tell you a secret: I still have Bobby! Today, I am in my late fifties, married, with six children, a bunch of grandchildren, and a raggedy childhood teddy bear. When I say raggedy, I mean my bear's fur has rubbed off in several places and his eyes are crooked. Why? Because one eye came off (oh, the horror!) and I had to ask my mom to sew it back on, which she did with only moderate success. Bobby's nose was supposed to be black. But the reason it's still black is because I used a Magic Marker to re-blacken it (when I was a kid, not recently).

Bobby and I had a lot of great years together.

Today, if I tried to sell my bear at a garage sale, I doubt it would bring even a quarter.

My bear may be a mess, but I love my bear! And who is Bobby valuable to? Me! Ask me its worth and my answer is "Priceless." Perhaps no one else can see it, but I do. I don't love Bobby because he's valuable. I love Bobby because he is *my* bear. My love gives him value.

That is exactly how God loves you.

Did you get that? It is the most life-changing truth bomb, so let me have you read it again: That is how God loves *you*.

Like me, you are flawed. You are broken. You are wounded. You may not feel attractive, athletic, talented, or smart enough. Doesn't matter. You may be a raggedy old bear, but you are God's raggedy old bear.

You may not feel valuable enough to love, but that doesn't affect God's love for you. God's love is the second kind of love, which means his love *gives* you value. He loves you not because you are worthy but because you are his.

And God set the price tag on your life, demonstrating how valuable you are, by giving up what was most valuable to him. That's what we read in Romans 5:6–8. If you'll give me a little leeway, here's my very loose paraphrase of that passage: "You see, at just the right time, when we were a hot mess nobody would've thought was worth a thing, Christ died for the extremely messy. Very rarely will anyone give something significant for someone insignificant, though for a significant person someone might possibly dare to do so. But God demonstrates how valuable he finds us in this: While we were still without value, he gave what was most valuable—Jesus—for us."

> **GOD LOVES YOU NOT BECAUSE YOU ARE WORTHY BUT BECAUSE YOU ARE HIS.**

Our first distorted belief is "But I'm too insignificant." Our second is "But I'm too sinful."

But I'm Too Sinful

The common belief is "I'm too sinful to be loved by God."

I've heard it. So many times.

I've felt it. So many times.

But when we doubt that God could love us because of our sin, we're either not understanding his love or we're forgetting something about his love. Why? Because God's love not only gives us value but also covers our sin. As 1 Peter 4:8 says, "Love covers a multitude of sins" (ESV).

If you wonder what "covers our sin" means or why this is important, here's an analogy: You and a friend go on a trip, and on the first day at the first stop, you reach for your wallet. It's not there. You look through everything and it is nowhere to be found. You panic and say, "Oh no, everything I need, all the costs on this trip, I can't pay. What am I going to do?" Your friend says, "Hey, don't worry another minute. I've got you." And what does your friend say next? "I've got you covered."

When we could not possibly pay the debt of our sin, Jesus covered us. His sacrifice on the cross and resurrection made a way.

How amazing is that? God doesn't just love us despite our sin; his love is so powerful it *covers* our sin. That's why Jesus came for us. That's what he came to do. "This is how God showed his love among us: He sent his one and only Son into the world that we might live through him. This is love: not that we loved God, but that he loved us and sent his Son as an atoning sacrifice for our sins" (1 John 4:9–10).

When we put our faith in Jesus' sacrifice, he atones for our sins, which means he covers our sins. That means God doesn't hold our sins against us.

These verses are powerful, but maybe even more so when you think about who wrote them. John was one of Jesus' disciples, but no one would have considered him to be disciple material. He and his brother James, whom Jesus also chose, did not

- graduate at the top of their class.
- make the best-behaved list.
- earn merit badges from the local rabbi.

There's a good chance that John and James were brash, rough, and loud. I bet they cursed up a storm. Speaking of storms, Jesus gave them a nickname. Not the "Bible Brothers" or the "Sweet Siblings." Mark 3:17 says, "To them he gave the name Boanerges, which means 'sons of thunder.'" Sounds like a pro-wrestling tag team. (Maybe that's where "Let's get ready to rumble!" started?) You don't get called that nickname because you wear pastel-colored sweater vests and penny loafers, drive a Vespa, and enjoy avocado toast. I'm seeing two guys who wear leather, drive Harleys, and get into bar fights. (Maybe even take a swing at an angry street preacher.)

We don't know for sure why Jesus called them the Sons of Thunder, but we get a pretty good hint in Luke 9. Jesus went into a town and we're told that the people there "did not welcome him" (v. 53). The next verse tells us what the Sons of Thunder said in response. Here's what they didn't say: "Let's make them some brownies! We'll kill 'em with kindness!" Nope. They said, "Lord, do you want us to call fire down from heaven to destroy them?" (v. 54). They did not want to kill people with kindness, they just wanted to kill them! (You know two guys are confident when they think they can call down fire!)

That's the Sons of Thunder. They found trouble wherever they went, and if they couldn't find it, they created it.

John, who was one of those bombastic brothers, had a sin problem. And so I imagine he was beyond shocked when Jesus chose him to be one of his followers. He probably just couldn't understand how Jesus—God in the flesh—could love him despite his sins. Until finally, three years later, he was standing next to Jesus' mother at the foot of the cross. I wonder whether he thought, *I get it now. God showed his love—even for sinners like me—by sending Jesus to be our atoning sacrifice. He's dying to cover my sins. That's how much God loves me.*

And that's also how much God loves you.

Love Is Who God Is

I was on an airplane having a nice conversation with the guy next to me. We were getting along great when he asked the dreaded question, "So what do you do for a living?"

Why is that such an awful question?

Because the reactions I get when I tell someone I'm a pastor are not too dissimilar from the ones I'd get if I answered, "You know those scam emails you get from a Nigerian prince? I'm the guy who sends those."

After a foreboding sigh, I responded, "Well, I'm a pastor of a church."

I hoped he might surprise me with "A pastor? That's awesome. Because I don't believe in God, but I want to! Could you explain Jesus and what he did on the cross for me? And if there's water on this plane, maybe you could baptize me."

He didn't.

Just as I suspected, his countenance immediately changed, and he said, "Well, I want you to know I don't believe in God. So don't talk to me about him."

I nodded. "Got it. Fair enough."

"I don't think you understand," he spoke forcefully, "I said I don't believe in God, and I don't wanna talk about him."

Politely, I answered, "Yes, I heard you."

He wouldn't quit. "Hey, are you sure you heard what I said? Don't be pushing your religion on me. I don't believe in God."

I thought, *Well, for someone who doesn't want to talk about God, you won't stop talking about him.* So I said, as graciously as I could, "Why don't you tell me about the God you don't believe in?"

"I will!" he nearly shouted. "I don't believe in your narrow-minded and angry God who's just waiting for people to sin, and as soon as they do, he writes 'em off and starts waiting with great delight to send them to hell."

I waited a second to make sure his speech was over, then told him, "Well, I don't believe in that God either."

I couldn't tell whether he was more surprised or suspicious, but he asked, "Huh? What do you mean?"

"When I read the Bible, I find a God who loves you. And maybe you've heard that before. Maybe you've heard that your whole life. Well, it's true. But it's even bigger than that. Way bigger. Because God doesn't just love you. God *is* love. Love is not just something God does. Love is who God is."

Isn't that incredible?

God *is* love. Just like one of the Sons of Thunder told us in 1 John 4:8, "God is love."

> LOVE IS NOT JUST SOMETHING GOD DOES. LOVE IS WHO GOD IS.

That means love is not just a characteristic of God. Take me, for example. When you ask people who know me, they might tell you, "Craig is loving." But I am not always loving. Let's just say I have my non-loving moments.

Not only is God loving, he *is* love. That means he is always loving. It is the essence of who he is. There's never a moment when he isn't love.

God is love. That means everything he says and everything he does flows from love. Because love is what he is.

First Corinthians 13 is often called the Love Chapter because in it Paul gives us our goal for the way we should love others in and through Christ. But there is only one who got this perfect every moment of every day of his life. The same one who loves you today. Because Jesus is patient and kind, doesn't envy, doesn't boast, isn't proud, doesn't dishonor others, isn't self-seeking, isn't easily angered, and—here's some great news—keeps no record of wrongs. He always protects, always trusts, always hopes, always perseveres. His love never fails (vv. 4–8).

God is love, and his love for you is unconditional. It's not based on your meeting his standards. He is love and loves you when you meet the conditions and loves you the same when you don't meet the conditions. You can't earn his love and you also can't sin your way out of it. There's nothing you can do to make him love you more and nothing you can do to make him love you less. In fact, you can never be more loved than you are right now.

God is love, which means his love for you is indestructible, invincible, and inexhaustible. His love doesn't run away or run out, doesn't leave or get lost, doesn't blow up or give up. You can count on it completely. Paul also tells us this about Jesus' love:

Who shall separate us from the love of Christ? Shall trouble or hardship or persecution or famine or nakedness or danger or sword? As it is written:

"For your sake we face death all day long;
we are considered as sheep to be slaughtered."

No, in all these things we are more than conquerors through him who loved us. For I am convinced that neither death nor life, neither angels nor demons, neither the present nor the future, nor any powers, neither height nor depth, nor anything else in all creation, will be able to separate us from the love of God that is in Christ Jesus our Lord.

—ROMANS 8:35-39

The One Jesus Loves

When you can move past your doubts and accept God's love for you, it turns your life from upside down to right side up.

That's what it did for John.

One day on a beach Jesus invited John to follow him. John said yes and started spending all his days with Jesus. Jesus knew he was a Son of Thunder, and he knew what he had done, but he loved John. It was hard to believe at first, but over time it became undeniable and overwhelming. So much so that John's identity, the way he saw himself, changed.

How do we know?

Because five times in his gospel John referred to himself as "the disciple whom Jesus loved" (John 13:23; 19:26; 20:2; 21:7; 21:20).

He was no longer the punk kid, no longer the hothead, no longer the screw-up or the instigator. None of that mattered. That no longer defined him. He was the one Jesus loved.

The same is true of you.

No matter what your family said about you, no matter how the kids at school made you feel, no matter what your boss says, no matter what you've done . . .

You are the one Jesus loves.

You might want to stop reading for a moment, close your eyes, and say out loud, "I am the one Jesus loves." Say it with all the conviction you can muster, because it's true. "I am the one Jesus loves."

> YOU ARE THE ONE JESUS LOVES.

He loves you, and he came for you.

Jesus said if a shepherd has one hundred sheep and one wanders away, he will leave the ninety-nine to go after the one (Matt. 18:12–13).

Why?

Because he loves the missing one the same as the ninety-nine in the flock. Because he misses the missing one.

You are the one.

If you have wandered away from him, if your doubts have dragged you off into the distance, he misses you, and he's coming for you. He's coming for you because he loves you.

You are the one Jesus loves.

You Are the One

Now, let's go back to the story where I was standing outside the bar with Drunk Buddy, who I had to stop from trying to beat the tar out of Angry Street Preacher. (Which, looking back, might not have been the worst thing.) (I'm kidding!)

Drunk Buddy kept telling me that God didn't love him, and I kept insisting he did. "God loves you!"

"No, he doesn't."

"Yes, God loves you."

Suddenly I felt a leading from the Holy Spirit. I hurt for this guy and his belief that God couldn't love him. I felt prompted to just go with it and agree with him. Drunk Buddy cried, "No, he doesn't!"

And I said, "You know what? You may be right."

It was as if he half sobered up in a split second. "Huh? Wait. What did you say?"

"I said you're probably right. God probably doesn't love you."

He was confused. "Well, he might?"

"No," I told him. "No, God loves everyone else but not you. You are the exception. You've just sinned too much."

"But . . . but . . ." Drunk Buddy was changing his mind. "But God could forgive me."

I shook my head. "No, I don't think he will."

"What?! Why not? I think he could. God loves me and he'll forgive me. Because of Jesus, right?"

It was the most amazing thing I've ever seen. Drunk Buddy led himself to Christ! He shared the gospel with himself and then we prayed together for his salvation.

For years, he was convinced he was the exception to the truth about God's love. Until I helped him turn the tables to realize he was actually the one Jesus had come after.

I stayed in touch with the guy. (Who became just Buddy. No more Drunk.) Two years later, he was a volunteer youth pastor! His entire life was changed because he recognized that God doesn't just love, God *is* love, and that his love gives us value and covers a multitude of sins.

That's how God loves you.

You are not insignificant to him.

You are not too sinful for him to save.

I understand your doubts, but no matter who you are, no matter what you've done, I can assure you: you are the one.

You are the one Jesus would leave the ninety-nine for, to go in pursuit of.

You are the one he would go to the cross for, to atone for all your sins.

You are the one Jesus loves.

> And I pray that you, being rooted and established in love, may have power, together with all the Lord's holy people, to grasp how wide and long and high and deep is the love of Christ, and to know this love that surpasses knowledge—that you may be filled to the measure of all the fullness of God.
>
> —EPHESIANS 3:17–19

CHAPTER 10 EXERCISE

1. Why do you think the reality of our sin, regardless of what it may be, often causes us to question whether we can be loved by God?

2. Has there ever been a time in your life when you felt as though you were the exception to God's love and he couldn't possibly love you? Explain. What about today?

3. How much have you struggled with feeling too insignificant? How has that feeling affected your relationship with God?

4. What are your thoughts on the first type of love: "A love that loves because the object is valuable"?

5. Why do you think this type of love has become so increasingly prevalent in our culture with so many people feeling as if they aren't attractive, athletic, talented, or smart enough?

6. What are your thoughts on the second type of love, which "gives value to the object being loved"?

7. How might you better embrace the truth that God's love is what gives you value?

8. Have you struggled with the Bible teaching that God's love covers your sins? If so, how? If not, why not?

9. Is it helpful to personalize the gospel by realizing that you are the one Jesus went to the cross for, and you are the one Jesus loves? Explain.

10. What was your main takeaway from this chapter?

Conclusion

GIVING GOD THE BENEFIT OF THE DOUBT

Imagine you're sitting at a restaurant where you're supposed to be meeting a friend for lunch. You're looking at your phone when you realize ten minutes have gone by. Your friend is late. You keep checking your phone for a text or call. Nothing. Your friend is now twenty minutes late and you haven't heard a word. You come to the conclusion you've been stood up.

Question: What do you think of your friend?

Answer: It depends on which friend it is.

Right?

With some friends you'd think, "Unbelievable! No, this is *totally* believable. He is so unreliable. And inconsiderate. Why'd I even think he'd show up?"

You would have real doubts about that friend.

But with other friends you'd think, "Wow, this is so unlike her. Maybe she's sick? But she would have called. I hope she didn't get in a car accident."

You would give that friend the benefit of the doubt.

The way you'd react would depend on which friend was supposed to meet you.

And you also wouldn't decide what you thought about your friend in that moment. Your reaction would have been established prior to that.

Your response would have been set by what you already believed about your friend.

In the Old Testament story of Job, he loses everything. He is distraught and confused and, understandably, he starts questioning God. But while he struggles with doubt, he gives God the benefit of the doubt. In the middle of unbearable pain, he holds on to his faith and declares boldly, "Though he slay me, yet will I hope in him" (Job 13:15), and "I know that my redeemer lives, and that in the end he will stand on the earth" (Job 19:25).

I love that Job had doubts (just as we all do at times), but he didn't allow his doubts to define God. Job had doubts, but he still trusted him, because he didn't define God in those moments. He had already decided what he believed.

As we read Job's story, we can tell that he had spent his life getting to know God. He had a real relationship in which he knew God.

And because he had already decided who God was, when he was hit by hard times and troubling doubts, Job could still give him the benefit of the doubt.

How about you?

When struggles, questions, and doubts come, do you define God only by those moments?

The good news is that no matter your answer, you can, like Job, give God the benefit of the doubt.

Because we all struggle with doubts. We've learned that it's completely normal to have questions. Just as Job did, we should feel free to ask away. But at the same time we can give God the benefit of the doubt.

Answers or the Answer

I find it fascinating that Job asked God questions and God showed up.

But God didn't give Job any answers. In fact, he asked Job a bunch of rhetorical questions of his own.

It reminds me of another moment in the Bible.

In John 11, someone informs Jesus that his good friend Lazarus is sick. Lazarus is the brother of Mary and Martha, who are also close friends of Jesus. The sisters' message to Jesus in verse 3 is, "Lord, the one you love is sick." Though Lazarus is on his deathbed, Jesus delays departing for several days. Finally, he makes the trip to the town where Lazarus lives. Jesus arrives to discover Lazarus is already dead.

Jesus is greeted by Lazarus' grieving sister Mary. We're told she is weeping, and others who were with her were also crying. Mary blurts out her complaint to Jesus: "If you had been here, my brother would not have died" (v. 21).

Mary hits Jesus with a stinging accusation. "Jesus, why did you allow this?" Everyone is hurting, confused, and overflowing with questions. "Couldn't you have prevented this?" Maybe even though no one said it, they may have been thinking, *Don't you care?*

Surprisingly, Jesus doesn't answer their questions.

I'm not sure why. Because there were answers. He could have explained that he delayed so Lazarus would die, so he could raise him from the dead. Which was about to happen in sixty seconds, fifty-nine, fifty-eight, fifty-seven. And because Jesus miraculously raised Lazarus, there would be other people who would come to faith. But Jesus didn't give any answers.

When he can, why doesn't he?

Why doesn't God explain everything to us?

Maybe it's because the answers are beyond us. Or perhaps Jesus is trying to build our faith. Or, even more likely, it's because there are some things we could never fully understand even if God himself were to explain them to us.

> MAYBE GOD DOESN'T EXPLAIN EVERYTHING BECAUSE THE ANSWERS ARE BEYOND US.

Jesus didn't give answers. So what did he do?

He showed up.

Job wanted answers. God gave him *the* answer. He gave Job himself.

God showed up, and God's presence was enough for Job.

Why? Because of their relationship.

In the same way, God's presence can be enough for you.

Just as Job had to decide, so do you.

The Third Option

Thank you for sticking with me all the way to the end. The fact that you stayed with a whole book on spiritual doubts says a lot about you. You're obviously serious about your relationship with God. In case you don't recognize it, that's something special. Yet even after reading this book, you likely still have unanswered questions. Chances are you will always have questions.

WHEN YOU MAY NOT HAVE ALL THE ANSWERS, YOU STILL HAVE GOD.

You want answers.

You ask God for them.

And he offers himself.

You may not have all the answers, but you have God.

What exactly are you supposed to do with him?

You habakkuk.

Somewhere toward the end of the Old Testament, where guys with unusual names like Obadiah and Nahum and Haggai hang out, you find Habakkuk.

Habakkuk was a prophet during a time when God's people weren't really following God. They had become evil, corrupt, and wicked. God told Habakkuk that because of their wickedness he was going to use people who were even more evil to punish them.

Habakkuk was not happy.

We see him spend a lot of time alternating between complaining and questioning. The book begins with Habakkuk shouting to the heavens, "How long, LORD, must I call for help, but you do not listen? Or cry out to you, 'Violence!' but you do not save? Why do you make me look at injustice? Why do you tolerate wrongdoing? Destruction and violence are before me; there is strife, and conflict abounds" (Hab. 1:2–3).

He was asking honestly, "God, how long do I have to see all of this injustice in the world? You could do something. But you don't."

What do you do when you feel that way?

When you have questions but no answers?

When you want to trust God, but he doesn't seem to be doing what you think he should do.

Typically, you make one of two choices:

1. You deny your faith.
2. You deny your questions.

With choice one, you decide you're done with God. You tried to trust him. You prayed your prayers. You went to church. You trusted his people. And he let you down. So you walk away. You deny your faith and stop believing in a God who didn't come through for you in the way you thought he should.

With choice two, you deny your questions. You push them down and pretend as if they aren't there. You do your best to keep on believing even though you've got doubts lurking in the back of your mind. You have questions you dare not ask.

Though both options feel tempting at times, neither will lead you where you want to go.

So I've got good news. There's a third option. It's the much better, but more difficult, path.

The third option is to choose to say, "God, I'm still going to trust you. Even if it doesn't make sense to me. Even if I don't like it. I'm going to give you the benefit of the doubt."

If you make that faith-filled decision, God can take you to a deep and intimate place.

To be clear, I'm not saying if you make this decision, things will get better immediately. They may get worse. And you may even continue to struggle with your faith.

But if you continue to pursue God one day at a time (just as you've been doing in your journey through this book one page at a time), he'll take you to a place of greater trust, stronger faith, and deeper intimacy with him than you've ever had before.

But, to get there, you must have the courage to live in the tension of this third option.

That's what Habakkuk did. Read his book in the Bible and you'll see him both trusting God and questioning God.

That's why his name is so perfect. You know how names mean something?

My name, Craig, derives from the Scottish Gaelic word *creag* and means "rock." My wife Amy's name is a form of the Latin name Amata and means "beloved." My sons Stephen's and Samuel's names mean "crowned one" and "God has heard." My daughter Joy's name means, well, joy.

The name Habakkuk means "to wrestle" or "to embrace."

It can mean either. And it means both.

And that is exactly what Habakkuk did.

He wrestled with God.

He embraced God.

He had both faith and questions. Both/and.

And remember—Habakkuk was the person God chose to be his prophet. To be the one who represented and spoke for him. He was someone God honored.

He didn't think faith was easy. He didn't have a smug or naive spiritual confidence or wear a T-shirt that read, "God said it. I believe it. That settles it."

I'm not sure whether Habakkuk was into faith-based casual clothing, but if he were, I think his T-shirt would have read, "I don't get it. I don't like it. But I'm trying to trust God anyway."

That probably wouldn't be a bestselling shirt today, but it's where Habakkuk was at, and it's how I often feel. So I want you to know you can have both faith and questions at the same time. You can wrestle with God *and* embrace him.

Who Are You Embracing?

If you choose to take this third option, who exactly would you be embracing?

You'd be embracing the God who created you, because he loved the idea of you and wanted to love you and for the world to know you.

The God who spoke and created a beautiful world for you to enjoy, filling it with more than four hundred thousand types of flowers for you to look at and eighty types of Oreos for you to eat. (Not to mention 18 decillion—that's an 18 followed by thirty-three zeros—colors for your viewing pleasure; almost 1.2 million mountains and hills for you to climb; more than ten thousand species of birds for those who enjoy looking at them; and I believe almost as many *Fast and Furious* movies for people who love Vin Diesel.)

The God who gave you the capacity to laugh when your friends tell dumb jokes and cry with them when they're hurting.

The God who, when you made self-destructive, sinful choices, rebelling against and wandering away from him, did not reject you but came to rescue you.

The God who, from the moment you were born, was loving you by working together each event in your life (including those you didn't want) for your good and for his glory.

The God who didn't impersonally shout his love from heaven but intimately showed his love on earth.

The God who surrendered the glory of all his eternal riches and chose to live a human life so he could understand what it's like to be you.

The God who, when he became a human, chose to be born to poor parents and live a life in which he would struggle with temptation and exhaustion and anxiety and be rejected by his friends. All so he could relate to you and be a compassionate source of strength when you're feeling fragile.

The God who touched lepers, gave sight to the blind, helped the lame dance, protected the weak, and fed the hungry.

The God who modeled a sympathetic, generous, sacrificial life of love here on this earth, and called his followers to imitate him.

The God who humbled himself and suffered the wrath of those he had created, to pay the penalty for their sins and for yours and mine.

That is the God you are embracing.

That is the God who is embracing you.

While you will never have all your questions answered this side of heaven, you can be sure of one thing.

You can give God the benefit of the doubt.

> **"I had only heard about you before, but now I have seen you with my own eyes."**
> —Job 42:5 NLT

CONCLUSION EXERCISE

1. Think back to the analogy about giving some friends the benefit of the doubt but not others. Before you read this book, was God the one you wouldn't give the benefit of the doubt or the one you would? Explain.
2. Considering the stories of Job and Lazarus, why do you think God would, at times, not offer you answers but simply show up and allow you to know his presence?
3. Do you agree with the statement "God's presence can be enough for you"? Why or why not?
4. Of the two choices of doubt—"Deny your faith" or "Deny your questions"—which one has been your tendency in the past? Explain.
5. Considering Habakkuk as an example, how is it possible that "you can wrestle with God *and* you can embrace him"?

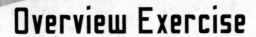

Overview Exercise

1. In contrast to before you began this book, where do you stand now on giving God the benefit of the doubt?
2. What Scripture verse or passage most affected you? Explain.
3. What was your biggest takeaway or "aha moment" in the book?
4. Is your perspective on dealing with doubts in your faith different now from when you started the book? Why or why not?
5. Have the points raised in this book about the hard questions of Christianity inspired you to make any changes in your approach to God or in your relationship with God through Jesus? Answer as specifically as possible.

Where Do I Go from Here?

After finishing this book and working through the exercises, if you have decided you are ready to reengage and reconstruct your relationship with God through Jesus Christ, here are a few simple steps you can take.

First, the most important decision in staying connected to your faith and growing consistently in maturity is to commit to the basics. Christians don't fall morally or walk away from their faith because they haven't resolved their end-times theology or can't correctly interpret the imagery in Revelation. They simply begin to ignore the basics, often to the point of abandoning them.

STAY CONNECTED TO GOD'S WORD, THE BIBLE. Whether you read one verse, a passage, or a chapter each day, be consistent. If you miss a day or two, no guilt, just jump back in. If you wonder where to start, the Gospel of John is a great launching point. Romans is also an amazing book to help you understand what we believe and why. Pray for God's Spirit to guide you as you read.

STAY CONNECTED TO PRAYER, YOUR LIFELINE TO GOD. Finding a time somewhere in the course of your day to talk with and listen to God is vitally important to maintain your relationship with your heavenly Father. There are no formulas or magic words to pray. Just be honest, be specific, and talk as if you are speaking with your best friend. Allowing some space to hear from God in your spirit is also important. While having a dedicated time to pray is good, throughout your day you can also whisper brief prayers for guidance, strength, and answers.

STAY CONNECTED TO COMMUNITY, A GROUP OF CHRIST FOLLOWERS. From the nation of Israel to the early church in Acts, it is clear that God created us to live and thrive in community. Being connected to a body of believers is important to accelerate your spiritual maturity, as well as to fulfill your calling. Even Jesus had his twelve, along with the many who followed and fellowshiped with him. Discovering your place in the body of Christ through the leadership of the Holy Spirit can keep you tethered to your brothers and sisters who love Jesus and who love you and need your love.

Appendix

Be strong and courageous. Do not be afraid; do not be discouraged, for the LORD your God will be with you wherever you go."

—Joshua 1:9

Though he slay me, yet will I hope in him."

—Job 13:15

I know that my redeemer lives, and that in the end he will stand on the earth."

—Job 19:25

I know the LORD is always with me. I will not be shaken, for he is right beside me. No wonder my heart is glad, and I rejoice. . . . You will show me the way of life, granting me the joy of your presence and the pleasures of living with you forever.

—Psalm 16:8–9, 11 NLT

The heavens proclaim the glory of God. The skies display his craftsmanship. Day after day they continue to speak; night after night they make him known. They speak without a sound or word; their voice is never heard. Yet their message has gone throughout the earth, and their words to all the world.

—Psalm 19:1–4 NLT

The instructions of the LORD are perfect, reviving the soul. The decrees of the LORD are trustworthy, making wise the simple. The commandments of the LORD are right, bringing joy to the heart. The commands of the LORD are clear, giving insight for living. . . . The laws of the LORD are true; each one is fair. They are more desirable than gold, even the finest gold. They are sweeter than honey, even honey dripping from the comb.

—Psalm 19:7–10 NLT

The LORD is my shepherd, I lack nothing. He makes me lie down in green pastures, he leads me beside quiet waters, he refreshes my soul. He guides me along the right paths for his name's sake. Even though I walk through the darkest valley, I will fear no evil, for you are with me.

—Psalm 23:1–4

The LORD is my light and my salvation—whom shall I fear? The LORD is the stronghold of my life—of whom shall I be afraid?

—Psalm 27:1

The righteous cry out, and the LORD hears them; he delivers them from all their troubles.

—Psalm 34:17

God is our refuge and strength, an ever-present help in trouble.

—Psalm 46:1

Yet I am always with you; you hold me by my right hand. You guide me with your counsel, and afterward you will take me into glory. . . . But as for me, it is good to be near God.

—Psalm 73:23–24, 28

As a father has compassion on his children, so the LORD has compassion on those who fear him; for he knows how we are formed, he remembers that we are dust.

—Psalm 103:13–14

Our help is in the name of the LORD, the Maker of heaven and earth.

—Psalm 124:8

The LORD is near to all who call on him, to all who call on him in truth. He fulfills the desires of those who fear him; he hears their cry and saves them.

—Psalm 145:18–19

Trust in the LORD with all your heart and lean not on your own understanding; in all your ways submit to him, and he will make your paths straight.

—Proverbs 3:5–6

There is a time for everything . . . a time to tear down and a time to build.

—Ecclesiastes 3:1, 3

So do not fear, for I am with you; do not be dismayed, for I am your God. I will strengthen you and help you; I will uphold you with my righteous right hand."

—Isaiah 41:10

So is my word that goes out from my mouth: It will not return to me empty, but will accomplish what I desire and achieve the purpose for which I sent it."

—Isaiah 55:11

For I know the plans I have for you," declares the LORD, "plans to prosper you and not to harm you, plans to give you hope and a future. Then you will call on me and come and pray to me, and I will listen to you. You will seek me and find me when you seek me with all your heart. I will be found by you," declares the LORD.

—Jeremiah 29:11-14

Therefore, if you are offering your gift at the altar and there remember that your brother or sister has something against you, leave your gift there in front of the altar. First go and be reconciled to them; then come and offer your gift."

—Matthew 5:23-24

But seek first his kingdom and his righteousness, and all these things will be given to you as well. Therefore do not worry about tomorrow, for tomorrow will worry about itself. Each day has enough trouble of its own."

—Matthew 6:33-34

Ask and it will be given to you; seek and you will find; knock and the door will be opened to you. For everyone who asks receives; the one who seeks finds; and to the one who knocks, the door will be opened."

—Matthew 7:7-8

Therefore everyone who hears these words of mine and puts them into practice is like a wise man who built his house on the rock. The rain came down, the streams rose, and the winds blew and beat against that house;

yet it did not fall, because it had its foundation on the rock. But everyone who hears these words of mine and does not put them into practice is like a foolish man who built his house on sand. The rain came down, the streams rose, and the winds blew and beat against that house, and it fell with a great crash."

—Matthew 7:24-27

Shortly before dawn Jesus went out to them, walking on the lake. . . . Jesus immediately said to them: "Take courage! It is I. Don't be afraid." "Lord, if it's you," Peter replied, "tell me to come to you on the water." "Come," he said. Then Peter got down out of the boat, walked on the water and came toward Jesus. But when he saw the wind, he was afraid and, beginning to sink, cried out, "Lord, save me!" Immediately Jesus reached out his hand and caught him. "You of little faith," he said, "why did you doubt?"

—Matthew 14:25-31

Jesus looked at them and said, "With man this is impossible, but with God all things are possible."

—Matthew 19:26

When they saw him, they worshiped him; but some doubted. Then Jesus came to them and said, "All authority in heaven and on earth has been given to me. Therefore go and make disciples of all nations, baptizing them in the name of the Father and of the Son and of the Holy Spirit, and teaching them to obey everything I have commanded you. And surely I am with you always, to the very end of the age."

—Matthew 28:17-20

If you can'?" said Jesus. "Everything is possible for one who believes." Immediately the boy's father exclaimed, "I do believe; help me overcome my unbelief!"

—Mark 9:23-24

Therefore I tell you, whatever you ask for in prayer, believe that you have received it, and it will be yours. And when you stand praying, if you hold anything against anyone, forgive them, so that your Father in heaven may forgive you your sins."

—Mark 11:24–25

Do not let your hearts be troubled. You believe in God; believe also in me."

—John 14:1

And I will ask the Father, and he will give you another advocate to help you and be with you forever."

—John 14:16

But when he, the Spirit of truth, comes, he will guide you into all the truth. He will not speak on his own; he will speak only what he hears, and he will tell you what is yet to come."

—John 16:13

Jesus] said to them . . . "Now is your time of grief, but I will see you again and you will rejoice, and no one will take away your joy."

—John 16:19, 22

I have told you these things, so that in me you may have peace. In this world you will have trouble. But take heart! I have overcome the world."

—John 16:33

Now Thomas (also known as Didymus), one of the Twelve, . . . said to them, "Unless I see the nail marks in his hands and put my finger where the nails were, and put my hand into his side, I will not believe." A week later . . . Jesus came and stood among them and said, "Peace be with you!" Then he said to Thomas, "Put your finger here; see my hands.

Reach out your hand and put it into my side. Stop doubting and believe."
Thomas said to him, "My Lord and my God!" Then Jesus told him,
"Because you have seen me, you have believed; blessed are those who
have not seen and yet have believed."

—John 20:24–29

God did this so that they would seek him and perhaps reach out for him
and find him, though he is not far from any one of us."

—Acts 17:27

For ever since the world was created, people have seen the earth and
sky. Through everything God made, they can clearly see his invisible
qualities—his eternal power and divine nature. So they have no excuse
for not knowing God.

—Romans 1:20 NLT

Christ died for us at a time when we were helpless and sinful. No one
is really willing to die for an honest person, though someone might be
willing to die for a truly good person. But God showed how much he
loved us by having Christ die for us, even though we were sinful. But
there is more! Now that God has accepted us because Christ sacrificed
his life's blood, we will also be kept safe from God's anger.

—Romans 5:6–9 CEV

Therefore, there is now no condemnation for those who are in Christ
Jesus.

—Romans 8:1

In the same way, the Spirit helps us in our weakness. We do not know
what we ought to pray for, but the Spirit himself intercedes for us
through wordless groans. . . . And we know that in all things God works
for the good of those who love him, who have been called according to
his purpose. . . . What, then, shall we say in response to these things?

If God is for us, who can be against us? He who did not spare his own Son, but gave him up for us all—how will he not also, along with him, graciously give us all things?

—Romans 8:26, 28, 31–32

Who shall separate us from the love of Christ? Shall trouble or hardship or persecution or famine or nakedness or danger or sword? As it is written: "For your sake we face death all day long; we are considered as sheep to be slaughtered." No, in all these things we are more than conquerors through him who loved us. For I am convinced that neither death nor life, neither angels nor demons, neither the present nor the future, nor any powers, neither height nor depth, nor anything else in all creation, will be able to separate us from the love of God that is in Christ Jesus our Lord.

—Romans 8:35–39

So faith comes from hearing, that is, hearing the Good News about Christ.

—Romans 10:17 NLT

For we live by faith, not by sight.

—2 Corinthians 5:7

Therefore, if anyone is in Christ, the new creation has come: The old has gone, the new is here!

—2 Corinthians 5:17

But he said to me, "My grace is sufficient for you, for my power is made perfect in weakness." Therefore I will boast all the more gladly about my weaknesses, so that Christ's power may rest on me. That is why, for Christ's sake, I delight in weaknesses, in insults, in hardships, in persecutions, in difficulties. For when I am weak, then I am strong."

—2 Corinthians 12:9–10

I have been crucified with Christ and I no longer live, but Christ lives in me. The life I now live in the body, I live by faith in the Son of God, who loved me and gave himself for me.

—Galatians 2:20

Do not be anxious about anything, but in every situation, by prayer and petition, with thanksgiving, present your requests to God.

—Philippians 4:6

Yet now he has reconciled you to himself through the death of Christ in his physical body. As a result, he has brought you into his own presence, and you are holy and blameless as you stand before him without a single fault.

—Colossians 1:22 NLT

Since you have been raised to new life with Christ, set your sights on the realities of heaven, where Christ sits in the place of honor at God's right hand. Think about the things of heaven, not the things of earth.

—Colossians 3:1–2 NLT

And we also thank God continually because, when you received the word of God, which you heard from us, you accepted it not as a human word, but as it actually is, the word of God, which is indeed at work in you who believe.

—1 Thessalonians 2:13

For the Spirit God gave us does not make us timid, but gives us power, love and self-discipline.

—2 Timothy 1:7

Now faith is confidence in what we hope for and assurance about what we do not see.

—Hebrews 11:1

And without faith it is impossible to please God, because anyone who comes to him must believe that he exists and that he rewards those who earnestly seek him.

—Hebrews 11:6

Let us draw near to God with a sincere heart and with the full assurance that faith brings. . . . Let us hold unswervingly to the hope we profess, for he who promised is faithful.

—Hebrews 10:22-23

God has said, "Never will I leave you; never will I forsake you." So we say with confidence, "The Lord is my helper; I will not be afraid."

—Hebrews 13:5-6

If any of you lacks wisdom, you should ask God, who gives generously to all without finding fault, and it will be given to you.

—James 1:5

You do not have because you do not ask God. When you ask, you do not receive, because you ask with wrong motives, that you may spend what you get on your pleasures.

—James 4:2-3

Husbands, in the same way be considerate as you live with your wives, and treat them with respect as the weaker partner and as heirs with you of the gracious gift of life, so that nothing will hinder your prayers.

—1 Peter 3:7

Cast all your anxiety on him because he cares for you.

—1 Peter 5:7

The Lord is not slow in keeping his promise, as some understand slowness. Instead he is patient with you, not wanting anyone to perish, but everyone to come to repentance.

—2 Peter 3:9

If we confess our sins, he is faithful and just and will forgive us our sins and purify us from all unrighteousness.

—1 John 1:9

This is how God showed his love among us: He sent his one and only Son into the world that we might live through him. This is love: not that we loved God, but that he loved us and sent his Son as an atoning sacrifice for our sins.

—1 John 4:9-10

This is the confidence we have in approaching God: that if we ask anything according to his will, he hears us. And if we know that he hears us—whatever we ask—we know that we have what we asked of him.

—1 John 5:14-15

Be merciful to those who doubt.

—Jude 22

Look! God's dwelling place is now among the people, and he will dwell with them. They will be his people, and God himself will be with them and be their God."

—Revelation 21:3

He who was seated on the throne said, "I am making everything new!" Then he said, "Write this down, for these words are trustworthy and true."

—Revelation 21:5

I did not see a temple in the city, because the Lord God Almighty and the Lamb are its temple. The city does not need the sun or the moon to shine on it, for the glory of God gives it light, and the Lamb is its lamp.

—Revelation 21:22–23

Acknowledgments

I'd like to express my deepest gratitude to all my friends and family who helped make this book possible.

To Amy Groeschel: you are my best friend. Thank you for serving Jesus with me for all these years. I love you more today than ever.

Vince Antonucci: it's fun to see how our friendship has grown through the years. Every book you've touched is indescribably better because of your hard work, your ideas, and your heart for God and ministry. Thank you for sharing your gifts with me. You are the fastest and the best.

Robert Noland: after your help on the last several books, now I'm afraid to do one without you. Thank you for going deep into the manuscript to make it stronger and more applicable. Your heart for this message shows on every page.

Adrianne Manning: you are the "book whisperer." Your love for these ministry projects is unparalleled. Thank you for bringing your whole heart to make every word count to change lives. You are world class at what you do and a blast to work with.

James and Mandy Meehan: your passion for this subject helped more than you know. Thanks for caring about those who are struggling in their faith and helping to love them back to Jesus.

Katherine Fedor: thank you for catching all the mistakes that everyone else missed. Your eye for detail honors God and blesses me.

Jenn McCarty, Leanna Romoser, Emilee Rowles, Mark Dawson, Sam

Naifeh, Stu Adams: you all helped make this message stronger and will extend its reach significantly.

Webster Younce, Brian Phipps, Curt Diepenhorst, Katie Painter, and the whole team at Zondervan: it's truly an honor to publish with you. You are mission minded in all you do and I'm grateful for our publishing partnership.

Tom Winters: you're a dang good agent. Thank you for navigating all the complexities of publishing and for working hard to reach more people through the written word.

To you, the reader: thank you for taking this journey with me. I pray that you continue to pursue Jesus, serve Jesus, and glorify Jesus. No matter what happens or how life hits you, remember, Jesus will never leave you.

Notes

Chapter 2: Is There Life after Deconstruction?

1. Lizzy Haseltine, "What Is Deconstruction?" Lifeway Research, October 19, 2022, https://research.lifeway.com/2022/10/19/what-is-deconstruction/.
2. Philip Yancey, *Where the Light Fell: A Memoir* (Colorado Springs: Convergent, 2023), 33.
3. Yancey, *Where the Light Fell*, 141.
4. Yancey, *Where the Light Fell*, 204.
5. Randy Frazee, *Think, Act, Be Like Jesus: Becoming a New Person in Christ* (Grand Rapids: Zondervan, 2014), 16–17.

Chapter 3: Why Should I Believe God Is Good?

1. Robert Burk, "The Epicurean Paradox Unpacked," ResearchGate, May 2023, www.researchgate.net/publication/371166291_The_Epicurean _Paradox_Unpacked.
2. Scot McKnight, *The Jesus Creed: Loving God, Loving Others* (Brewster, MA: Paraclete, 2004), 263.
3. John Goldingay, quoted in Scot McKnight, *The Jesus Creed: Loving God, Loving Others* (Brewster, MA: Paraclete, 2004), 263.

Chapter 4: Why Doesn't God Answer My Prayers?

1. "Reflections: Where Is God in the Silence?" C. S. Lewis Institute, July 1, 2008, www.cslewisinstitute.org/resources/reflections-july-2008/.
2. J. D. Greear, "Are You Praying Like an Adulterer?" Pastor Resources,

accessed June 14, 2024, https://pastorresources.com/answer-are-you
-praying-like-an-adulterer/.

3. Timothy Keller, *Prayer: Experiencing Awe and Intimacy with God* (New York: Penguin, 2014), 238.

Chapter 5: Why Would God Provide Only One Way?

1. "40 Quotes about the Life-Changing Power of the Resurrection," Communicate Jesus, accessed June 14, 2024, www.communicatejesus.com /post/40-quotes-life-changing-power-resurrection.

2. If you'd like to explore some of the evidence for Jesus' resurrection, you could check out books such as *The Case for the Resurrection of Jesus* by Gary Habermas and Michael Licona, *The Case for Easter* by Lee Strobel, and *The Resurrection of the Son of God* by N. T. Wright.

Chapter 6: Why Believe in Jesus When His Followers Are Such Hypocrites?

1. Will Heilpern, "Eighteen False Advertising Scandals That Cost Some Brands Millions," *Business Insider*, March 31, 2016, www.businessinsider .com/false-advertising-scandals-2016-3.

2. DC Talk, *Jesus Freaks* (Washington, DC: Eagle, 2004), 49.

3. Patrick Healy, "The Fundamental Attribution Error: What It Is and How to Avoid It," *Business Insights* (blog), Harvard Business School, June 8, 2017, https://online.hbs.edu/blog/post/the-fundamental-attribution-error.

Chapter 8: Why Would God Send People to Hell?

1. Mike Nappa, "What Did Jesus Say about Hell?" Christianity.com, September 5, 2023, www.christianity.com/wiki/heaven-and-hell/what-did -jesus-say-about-hell.html.

2. John Ortberg has some of the clearest and most compelling teachings I have heard on the subject of heaven and hell, and I am sharing some of his ideas. See, for example, his sermon "The Bad News about Heaven," ReGeneration Project, January 24, 2019, YouTube video, www.youtube .com/watch?v=bRKMd6V5AF8.

3. John Ortberg, *Eternity Is Now in Session: A Radical Rediscovery of What Jesus Really Taught about Salvation, Eternity, and Getting to the Good Place* (Carol Stream, IL: Tyndale, 2018), 12.

4. "Max Lucado: A Conversation about Hell," Life Today, March 18, 2022, YouTube video, www.youtube.com/watch?v=0JD6HZKj4gc.
5. David Platt, *Exalting Jesus in Matthew* (Brentwood, TN: Holman Bible Publishers, 2013), 223.

Chapter 9: Why Believe the Bible If Science Contradicts It?

1. "The Hall of Faith, Day 3 of 4: Trust God for the Unseen," Bible.com, accessed June 14, 2024, www.bible.com/reading-plans/18755-the-hall-of -faith/day/3.
2. Raymond Tallis, "Did Time Begin with a Bang?" *Philosophy Now*, 2012, https://philosophynow.org/issues/92/Did_Time_Begin_With_A_Bang.
3. Vicky Stein, "Einstein's Theory of Special Relativity," Space.com, February 1, 2022, www.space.com/36273-theory-special-relativity.html.
4. Hugh Ross, "Cosmology's Holy Grail," *Christianity Today*, December 12, 1994, www.christianitytoday.com/ct/1994/december12/4te024.html.
5. Hugh Ross, "Anthropic Principle: A Precise Plan for Humanity," Reasons to Believe, January 1, 2002, https://reasons.org/explore/publications/facts -for-faith/anthropic-principle-a-precise-plan-for-humanity.
6. David H. Bailey, "Is the Universe Fine-Tuned for Intelligent Life?" Math Scholar, April 1, 2017, https://mathscholar.org/2017/04/is-the -universe-fine-tuned-for-intelligent-life/#:~:text=Physicist%20Roger%20 Penrose%20has%20calculated,particles%20in%20the%20observable%20 universe.
7. Francis Collins, "Is There a God and Does He Care about Me?" BioLogos, December 16, 2019, https://biologos.org/personal-stories/is-there-a-god -and-does-he-care-about-me-the-testimony-of-biologos-founder-francis -collins.
8. Francis S. Collins, *The Language of God: A Scientist Presents Evidence for Belief* (New York: Free Press, 2006), 211.

Companion Workbook
Also Available

Doubt Isn't a Dead End

Find free, honest, and helpful resources at
finds.life.church

Dangerous Prayers

Because Following Jesus Was Never Meant to Be Safe

Craig Groeschel

Bestselling author Craig Groeschel helps you find the courage to dig yourself out of a spiritual rut and spark a new fire by praying three bold, specific prayers. Unlock your greatest potential and tackle your greatest fears by praying stronger, more passionate prayers, prayers that move the heart of God.

Hope in the Dark

Believing God Is Good When Life Is Not

Craig Groeschel

Sometimes it feels impossible to reconcile the pain of our circumstances with the image of an all-loving, all-powerful God. *Hope in the Dark* explores that poignant contradiction with gentle honesty, biblical truths, and stories of people who wrestled with deeply personal questions about God and faith.

Winning the War in Your Mind

Change Your Thinking, Change Your Life

Craig Groeschel

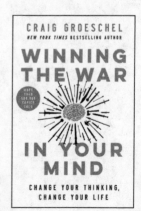

MORE THAN 500,000 COPIES SOLD!
Pastor and *New York Times* bestselling author Craig Groeschel provides four practical, life-changing strategies for breaking free from destructive thinking and for living the life God intends for you.

Available in stores and online!

Walk *Through* Doubt With God's Word.

You never have to face doubt alone. God's Word can help you navigate your questions and draw closer to the One who created you.

The Bible App from YouVersion offers over 60,000 Bible Plans, videos, and more, including content specifically on doubt—like *The Benefit of Doubt* Bible Plan.

Learn how to walk through doubt by discovering God's truth in His Word.

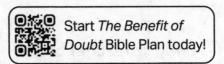

Start *The Benefit of Doubt* Bible Plan today!

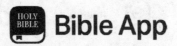

HOLY BIBLE **Bible App**

Additional Resources
to Grow in Your Faith

Get Craig's recommended reading list
by scanning the QR code above.

craiggroeschel.com

 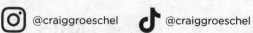